AMERICA'S #1 STANDARDS-BASED SCHOOL IMPROVEMENT PROGRAM

Day Two PSAE Victory

Student Textbook

Cambridge Publishing, Inc.
2720 River Road, Suite 36
Des Plaines, IL 60018
(847) 299-2930

Manufactured in the United States of America.
3 4 5 6 7 8 9 10
Edited by John R. Connolly, Jr., Thomas G. Jacobs, and David P. Waldherr.

Dear Student,

The fact that you're reading this book means just one thing—you've got a big, important test ahead of you. You want to do well, and we want to help you. This book will enable you not only to succeed on the Day Two PSAE, but also to improve your all-around academic performance and even to help provide skills that are directly applicable when you enter the workplace.

Since you began attending school, you've been taught thousands of things. No one expects you to remember every single concept that you've learned since you were five years old. However, the PSAE is a cumulative test, which means that you might be tested on concepts that you may have forgotten or that you may never have learned at all. Not only that, the PSAE tests these concepts in ways that most of your in-school tests never have—especially the Day Two PSAE tests, which focus on knowledge as it applies to the workplace.

This *Cambridge Day Two PSAE Victory Student Textbook* includes classroom lessons and practice problems for the material that you will encounter on the second day of PSAE testing: ISBE-Developed Science, WorkKeys Applied Mathematics, and WorkKeys Reading for Information. When paired with the *Cambridge ACT • PLAN • EXPLORE Victory Student Textbook*, you will have all of the materials that you need in order to: 1) refresh or build your understanding of important skills; 2) apply those skills in the particular context of the PSAE; and 3) reduce test anxiety through practice.

You have the tools to succeed. If you attend class, participate in learning, do all of your homework, and maintain a positive attitude, then you will do well on the PSAE.

Good Luck!

The Cambridge Curriculum Committee

Day Two PSAE

Table of Contents

STEP FOUR: PRACTICE TEST REINFORCEMENT

STEP FIVE: STANDARDS-BASED POST-ASSESSMENT, REPORT, AND REVIEW

STEP SIX: PERSONAL STUDY PLAN

ANSWER KEYS

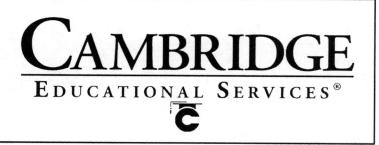

Day Two PSAE

INTRODUCTION

HOW TO USE THIS BOOK

This book is organized into six parts:

1) Forms that help you to make sense of your Day Two PSAE Mirror pre-test results (Step One);
2) Forms that help you to determine your strengths and weaknesses on the skills associated with the entire PSAE (Step Two);
3) Day Two PSAE problems resembling those on the real Day Two PSAE that your instructor will use to teach tested concepts and applicable strategies in the format of the real Day Two PSAE (Step Three);
4) Advice on where to find additional, official Day Two practice material (Step Four);
5) Forms that help you to make sense of your Day Two PSAE Mirror post-test results (Step Five); and
6) Forms that help you to determine what to do at the end of your Cambridge course to maximize your Day Two PSAE score (Step Six).

The following brief introduction will explain how to effectively use each part of this textbook.

UNDERSTANDING YOUR DAY TWO PSAE MIRROR PRE-TEST RESULTS

In order to know where to begin preparing for the Day Two PSAE, you first have to know what you already do well and what you could learn to do better. Step One serves this purpose. First, you will take a Day Two PSAE Mirror pre-test under actual testing conditions. Then, with the help of your instructor, you will use the results of this test to determine exactly which problems to review, how long to review them, and in what order to review them.

In Step One of this book, you will find progress report forms (pp. 13-23) on which you will record your results for the Day Two PSAE Mirror pre-test. Recording your results will help you to see your strengths and weaknesses more clearly.

Step One also contains a pre-test bubble sheet (p. 25), which you can use to respond to all areas of the pre-test.

DETERMINING YOUR PSAE STRENGTHS AND WEAKNESSES

Step Two contains progress report forms (pp. 33-43) that list every exercise in the Science Skills Review, Math Skills Review, and Reading Skills Review, which are located in the *Cambridge ACT • PLAN • EXPLORE Victory Student Textbook*. These forms provide a table for you to record how many problems you've completed and what percentage you've answered correctly. After you've completed each exercise, be sure to fill out the respective portion of the progress report. The form will document your progress and make it easier to recognize exactly what material in Step Three deserves most of your attention.

The Skills Review (Step Two) chapters found in the *Cambridge ACT • PLAN • EXPLORE Victory Student Textbook* contain problems that will enable you to do three things: 1) review material that you may have forgotten; 2) learn material that you may never have learned; and 3) master the skills that you need to answer the more difficult multiple-choice questions on both the ACT and the Day Two PSAE. The problems in these Skills Review chapters are at or below skill level so that you can use them to build fundamental skills.

These exercises do not necessarily contain problems that mimic PSAE problems. They are designed to help you to learn concepts—not necessarily to learn the particulars of the actual test. They are the foundation that you will need in order to take full advantage of the test-taking strategies and concepts developed in Step Three of this book. Your instructor may either review the Skills Review material in class or have you complete the exercises as homework.

SOLVING PROBLEMS LIKE THOSE FOUND ON THE TEST

Problem-solving, concepts, and strategies make up the heart of this course and, in particular, this textbook. Step Three contains problems that resemble those on the actual Day Two PSAE sections. When compared to problems on the actual test, the problems in this part of the book have similar content, represent the same difficulty range, and can be solved by using the same problem-solving skills and alternative test-taking strategies.

This part of the book is divided into three chapters; each chapter represents one of the Day Two PSAE test subject areas:

- ISBE-Developed Science
- Applied Mathematics
- Reading for Information

Each of these chapters is divided into three sections:

- Section One: Review
- Section Two: Problem-Solving
- Section Three: Quizzes

At the beginning of Step Three, there is a Cambridge Course Concept Outline. The outline acts as a course syllabus and lists the concepts that are tested for each problem-type. The problems in Section One are organized to correspond with the course concept outline. For each concept in the outline, there are various clusters of problems. Although the same concept is not necessarily tested consecutively on the real Day Two PSAE, Cambridge organizes the problems into clusters so that the concepts are emphasized and reinforced. Your instructor will use the Section One: Review problems to teach concepts and to demonstrate problem-solving techniques and alternative test-taking strategies for each of the three subject areas.

In Section Two, the problems are generally at a higher difficulty level; they give you a chance to apply the problem-solving techniques and alternative strategies that you learned in Section One: Review. Once you have mastered the concepts and strategies of the Day Two PSAE material in the first two sections, you will be ready to take on the added pressure of time limits in the Quizzes in Section Three.

Step Three also contains progress report forms (pp. 55-65) for each test section. These forms list every exercise in the Review, Problem-Solving, and Quizzes sections of this book, providing a table so that you may record how many problems you've completed and what percentage you've answered correctly. After you've completed each section of exercises, be sure to fill out the respective portion of the progress report. It will document your progress and make it easier to recognize exactly what test sections or specific problem-types deserve most of your attention when continuing your studies for the Day Two PSAE.

ADDITIONAL PRACTICE MATERIAL

In Step Four, you should practice applying the additional skills learned in Step Two and concepts and strategies learned in Step Three. You can find official practice items located online at the Illinois State Board of Education's Web site: isbe.net. You can download an informational guide as a PDF at the following web address: **www.isbe.net/assessment/psae.htm**. At the same address, you can also find a link to interactive sample items for not only the Day Two PSAE material, but also for the ACT, which is administered on the first day of the PSAE. Your instructor will ask you to complete some or all of these practice problems in class, or he or she will assign them as homework.

Four additional ACT Practice Tests are located in Step Four of the *Cambridge ACT • PLAN • EXPLORE Victory Student Textbook*. If you are taking these four tests at home, you should take two with time restrictions and two without time restrictions. Taking two tests without time restrictions will help you to get a sense of how long it would take for you to comfortably and accurately solve a problem. Applying time pressure for the other two tests then forces you to pace yourself as you would on the real test. If you complete all four of the practice tests, any test anxiety you may have will be greatly reduced.

Be sure to record your efforts on the progress report forms (pp. 161-175). These forms will be especially helpful after your course officially ends. At that point, you will make a plan for reviewing any areas in which you are still not performing as well as you would like.

MAKING SENSE OF YOUR DAY TWO PSAE MIRROR POST-TEST RESULTS

In order to know how far you've come since the pre-test, you have to take another Day Two PSAE Mirror test. Step Five serves this purpose. First, you will take the Day Two PSAE Mirror post-test under actual testing conditions. Then, you will use the results to evaluate your progress and to determine exactly which problems would be the most beneficial for you to review.

The Day Two PSAE Mirror post-test progress report forms (pp. 183-195) will help you make a personal study plan, so be sure to record your post-test results. In addition, Step Five contains a post-test bubble sheet (p. 195). You can use this sheet to respond to all areas of the post-test.

FIGURING OUT WHAT TO DO NEXT

The personal study plan progress report forms (pp. 205-207) will help you to create a prioritized list of what you still need to review before you take the actual Day Two PSAE. Each form asks you to rank your ability to solve problems in each test subject area and to specify the skills and strategies on which you should focus the most.

Even after your Cambridge course has finished, you will find that this book is a great resource for continued Day Two PSAE review and preparation.

STEP ONE: STANDARDS-BASED PRE-ASSESSSMENT AND REPORT

Day Two PSAE

STEP ONE: STANDARDS-BASED PRE-ASSESSMENT AND REPORT

AMERICA'S #1 STANDARDS-BASED SCHOOL IMPROVEMENT PROGRAM

Cambridge Course Concept Outline
STEP ONE

DAY TWO PSAE
MIRROR PRE-TEST PROGRESS REPORT
(Student Copy)

The Mirror Pre-Test Progress Reports are designed to help you make sense of your Day Two PSAE Mirror Pre-Test results. Your instructor will help you to target review areas and may assign additional skills reviews tailored to your abilities.

DIRECTIONS: Complete the diagnostic pre-test and record both the number and percentage of problems that you answered correctly. Identify the date on which you completed each section of the pre-test and list the numbers of any problems that you would like your instructor to review in class. If you are using the Cambridge Assessment Service, consult your PSAE Error Analysis for a breakdown of problems by category to complete the remainder of the form. Rank your weakest areas by category to identify weaknesses.

Transfer this information to the Instructor Copy, and then give that report to your instructor.

Name _____ Student ID _____ Date _____

ISBE-Developed Science
(Student Copy)

Date Completed: _____   Total # Possible: 45   # Correct: _____   % Correct: _____

Question Category	Total # Possible	# Correct	% Correct	Problem #s to Review	Rank
Biology					
Chemistry					
Earth					
Ecology					
Physics					
Society					
Space					

DAY TWO PSAE
MIRROR PRE-TEST PROGRESS REPORT
(Instructor Copy)

The Mirror Pre-Test Progress Reports are designed to help you make sense of your Day Two PSAE Mirror Pre-Test results. Your instructor will help you to target review areas and may assign additional skills reviews tailored to your abilities.

DIRECTIONS: Transfer the information from your Student Copy to the Instructor Copy below. Your instructor will use the last two bolded columns to evaluate your progress. Leave them blank. When finished, give this report to your instructor.

Name _____ Student ID _____ Date _____

ISBE-Developed Science
(Instructor Copy)

Date Completed: _____ Total # Possible: 45 # Correct: _____ % Correct: _____

Question Category	Total # Possible	# Correct	% Correct	Problem #s to Review	Rank	Instructor Skill Evaluation	
						Skills Review Needed? (Y or N)	*Skills Review Section and Problem Numbers Assigned*
Biology							
Chemistry							
Earth							
Ecology							
Physics							
Society							
Space							

DAY TWO PSAE
MIRROR PRE-TEST PROGRESS REPORT
(Student Copy)

The Mirror Pre-Test Progress Reports are designed to help you make sense of your Day Two PSAE Mirror Pre-Test results. Your instructor will help you to target review areas and may assign additional skills reviews tailored to your abilities.

DIRECTIONS: Complete the diagnostic pre-test and record both the number and percentage of problems that you answered correctly. Identify the date on which you completed each section of the pre-test and list the numbers of any problems that you would like your instructor to review in class. If you are using the Cambridge Assessment Service, consult your PSAE Error Analysis for a breakdown of problems by category to complete the remainder of the form. Rank your weakest areas by category to identify weaknesses.

Transfer this information to the Instructor Copy, and then give that report to your instructor.

Name _____ Student ID _____ Date _____

Applied Mathematics
(Student Copy)

Date Completed: _____ Total # Possible: 33 # Correct: _____ % Correct: _____

Question Category	Total # Possible	# Correct	% Correct	Problem #s to Review	Rank
Multi-Step Area/Perimeter					
Multi-Step Averages					
Multi-Step Best Deal					
Multi-Step Dimensional Analysis					
Multi-Step Mixed Units					
Multi-Step Rates					
Multi-Step Volumes					
Single-Step Area/Perimeter					
Single-Step Arithmetic					
Single-Step Averages					
Single-Step Best Deal					
Single-Step Dimensional Analysis					
Single-Step Mixed Units					
Single-Step Percent					

DAY TWO PSAE
MIRROR PRE-TEST PROGRESS REPORT

(Instructor Copy)

The Mirror Pre-Test Progress Reports are designed to help you make sense of your Day Two PSAE Mirror Pre-Test results. Your instructor will help you to target review areas and may assign additional skills reviews tailored to your abilities.

DIRECTIONS: Transfer the information from your Student Copy to the Instructor Copy below. Your instructor will use the last two bolded columns to evaluate your progress. Leave them blank. When finished, give this report to your instructor.

Name ______________________________ Student ID ______________ Date _____________

Applied Mathematics

(Instructor Copy)

Date Completed: ________________ Total # Possible: 33 # Correct: _______ % Correct: _______

						Instructor Skill Evaluation	
Question Category	***Total # Possible***	***# Correct***	***% Correct***	***Problem #s to Review***	***Rank***	***Review Needed? (Y or N)***	***Review Section and Problem Numbers Assigned***
Multi-Step Area/Perimeter							
Multi-Step Averages							
Multi-Step Best Deal							
Multi-Step Dimensional Analysis							
Multi-Step Mixed Units							
Multi-Step Rates							
Multi-Step Volumes							
Single-Step Area/Perimeter							
Single-Step Arithmetic							
Single-Step Averages							
Single-Step Best Deal							
Single-Step Dimensional Analysis							
Single-Step Mixed Units							
Single-Step Percent							

DAY TWO PSAE
MIRROR PRE-TEST PROGRESS REPORT
(Student Copy)

The Mirror Pre-Test Progress Reports are designed to help you make sense of your Day Two PSAE Mirror Pre-Test results. Your instructor will help you to target review areas and may assign additional skills reviews tailored to your abilities.

DIRECTIONS: Complete the diagnostic pre-test and record both the number and percentage of problems that you answered correctly. Identify the date on which you completed each section of the pre-test and list the numbers of any problems that you would like your instructor to review in class. If you are using the Cambridge Assessment Service, consult your PSAE Error Analysis for a breakdown of problems by category to complete the remainder of the form. Rank your weakest areas by category to identify weaknesses.

Transfer this information to the Instructor Copy, and then give that report to your instructor.

Name _____ Student ID _____ Date _____

Reading for Information
(Student Copy)

Date Completed: _____ Total # Possible: 33 # Correct: _____ % Correct: _____

Question Category	Total # Possible	# Correct	% Correct	Problem #s to Review	Rank
Author's Voice					
Cause/Effect					
Comparative Relationships					
Details					
Generalizations					
Main Idea					
Sequence					
Vocabulary					

DAY TWO PSAE
MIRROR PRE-TEST PROGRESS REPORT
(Instructor Copy)

The Mirror Pre-Test Progress Reports are designed to help you make sense of your Day Two PSAE Mirror Pre-Test results. Your instructor will help you to target review areas and may assign additional skills reviews tailored to your abilities.

DIRECTIONS: Transfer the information from your Student Copy to the Instructor Copy below. Your instructor will use the last two bolded columns to evaluate your progress. Leave them blank. When finished, give this report to your instructor.

Name _____ Student ID _____ Date _____

Reading for Information
(Instructor Copy)

Date Completed: _____ Total # Possible: 33 # Correct: _____ % Correct: _____

Question Category	Total # Possible	# Correct	% Correct	Problem #s to Review	Rank	Instructor Skill Evaluation	
						Skills Review Needed? (Y or N)	Skills Review Section and Problem Numbers Assigned
Author's Voice							
Cause/Effect							
Comparative Relationships							
Details							
Generalizations							
Main Idea							
Sequence							
Vocabulary							

Day Two PSAE Mirror Pre-Test Bubble Sheet

Name _____

Student ID Number _____

Date _____

Instructor _____

Course/Session Number _____

USE THIS BUBBLE SHEET ONLY IF YOU ARE NOT USING THE CAMBRIDGE ASSESSMENT REPORT SERVICE

MARK ONE AND ONLY ONE ANSWER TO EACH QUESTION. BE SURE TO COMPLETELY FILL IN THE SPACE FOR YOUR INTENDED ANSWER CHOICE. IF YOU ERASE, DO SO COMPLETELY. MAKE NO STRAY MARKS.

1 ISBE-Developed Science

1 Ⓐ Ⓑ Ⓒ Ⓓ	13 Ⓐ Ⓑ Ⓒ Ⓓ	25 Ⓐ Ⓑ Ⓒ Ⓓ	37 Ⓐ Ⓑ Ⓒ Ⓓ
2 Ⓕ Ⓖ Ⓗ Ⓙ	14 Ⓕ Ⓖ Ⓗ Ⓙ	26 Ⓕ Ⓖ Ⓗ Ⓙ	38 Ⓕ Ⓖ Ⓗ Ⓙ
3 Ⓐ Ⓑ Ⓒ Ⓓ	15 Ⓐ Ⓑ Ⓒ Ⓓ	27 Ⓐ Ⓑ Ⓒ Ⓓ	39 Ⓐ Ⓑ Ⓒ Ⓓ
4 Ⓕ Ⓖ Ⓗ Ⓙ	16 Ⓕ Ⓖ Ⓗ Ⓙ	28 Ⓕ Ⓖ Ⓗ Ⓙ	40 Ⓕ Ⓖ Ⓗ Ⓙ
5 Ⓐ Ⓑ Ⓒ Ⓓ	17 Ⓐ Ⓑ Ⓒ Ⓓ	29 Ⓐ Ⓑ Ⓒ Ⓓ	41 Ⓐ Ⓑ Ⓒ Ⓓ
6 Ⓕ Ⓖ Ⓗ Ⓙ	18 Ⓕ Ⓖ Ⓗ Ⓙ	30 Ⓕ Ⓖ Ⓗ Ⓙ	42 Ⓕ Ⓖ Ⓗ Ⓙ
7 Ⓐ Ⓑ Ⓒ Ⓓ	19 Ⓐ Ⓑ Ⓒ Ⓓ	31 Ⓐ Ⓑ Ⓒ Ⓓ	43 Ⓐ Ⓑ Ⓒ Ⓓ
8 Ⓕ Ⓖ Ⓗ Ⓙ	20 Ⓕ Ⓖ Ⓗ Ⓙ	32 Ⓕ Ⓖ Ⓗ Ⓙ	44 Ⓕ Ⓖ Ⓗ Ⓙ
9 Ⓐ Ⓑ Ⓒ Ⓓ	21 Ⓐ Ⓑ Ⓒ Ⓓ	33 Ⓐ Ⓑ Ⓒ Ⓓ	45 Ⓐ Ⓑ Ⓒ Ⓓ
10 Ⓕ Ⓖ Ⓗ Ⓙ	22 Ⓕ Ⓖ Ⓗ Ⓙ	34 Ⓕ Ⓖ Ⓗ Ⓙ	46 Ⓕ Ⓖ Ⓗ Ⓙ
11 Ⓐ Ⓑ Ⓒ Ⓓ	23 Ⓐ Ⓑ Ⓒ Ⓓ	35 Ⓐ Ⓑ Ⓒ Ⓓ	47 Ⓐ Ⓑ Ⓒ Ⓓ
12 Ⓕ Ⓖ Ⓗ Ⓙ	24 Ⓕ Ⓖ Ⓗ Ⓙ	36 Ⓕ Ⓖ Ⓗ Ⓙ	48 Ⓕ Ⓖ Ⓗ Ⓙ

2 Applied Mathematics

1 Ⓐ Ⓑ Ⓒ Ⓓ Ⓔ	10 Ⓕ Ⓖ Ⓗ Ⓙ Ⓚ	19 Ⓐ Ⓑ Ⓒ Ⓓ Ⓔ	28 Ⓕ Ⓖ Ⓗ Ⓙ Ⓚ
2 Ⓕ Ⓖ Ⓗ Ⓙ Ⓚ	11 Ⓐ Ⓑ Ⓒ Ⓓ Ⓔ	20 Ⓕ Ⓖ Ⓗ Ⓙ Ⓚ	29 Ⓐ Ⓑ Ⓒ Ⓓ Ⓔ
3 Ⓐ Ⓑ Ⓒ Ⓓ Ⓔ	12 Ⓕ Ⓖ Ⓗ Ⓙ Ⓚ	21 Ⓐ Ⓑ Ⓒ Ⓓ Ⓔ	30 Ⓕ Ⓖ Ⓗ Ⓙ Ⓚ
4 Ⓕ Ⓖ Ⓗ Ⓙ Ⓚ	13 Ⓐ Ⓑ Ⓒ Ⓓ Ⓔ	22 Ⓕ Ⓖ Ⓗ Ⓙ Ⓚ	31 Ⓐ Ⓑ Ⓒ Ⓓ Ⓔ
5 Ⓐ Ⓑ Ⓒ Ⓓ Ⓔ	14 Ⓕ Ⓖ Ⓗ Ⓙ Ⓚ	23 Ⓐ Ⓑ Ⓒ Ⓓ Ⓔ	32 Ⓕ Ⓖ Ⓗ Ⓙ Ⓚ
6 Ⓕ Ⓖ Ⓗ Ⓙ Ⓚ	15 Ⓐ Ⓑ Ⓒ Ⓓ Ⓔ	24 Ⓕ Ⓖ Ⓗ Ⓙ Ⓚ	33 Ⓐ Ⓑ Ⓒ Ⓓ Ⓔ
7 Ⓐ Ⓑ Ⓒ Ⓓ Ⓔ	16 Ⓕ Ⓖ Ⓗ Ⓙ Ⓚ	25 Ⓐ Ⓑ Ⓒ Ⓓ Ⓔ	34 Ⓕ Ⓖ Ⓗ Ⓙ Ⓚ
8 Ⓕ Ⓖ Ⓗ Ⓙ Ⓚ	17 Ⓐ Ⓑ Ⓒ Ⓓ Ⓔ	26 Ⓕ Ⓖ Ⓗ Ⓙ Ⓚ	35 Ⓐ Ⓑ Ⓒ Ⓓ Ⓔ
9 Ⓐ Ⓑ Ⓒ Ⓓ Ⓔ	18 Ⓕ Ⓖ Ⓗ Ⓙ Ⓚ	27 Ⓐ Ⓑ Ⓒ Ⓓ Ⓔ	36 Ⓕ Ⓖ Ⓗ Ⓙ Ⓚ

3 Reading for Information

1 Ⓐ Ⓑ Ⓒ Ⓓ Ⓔ	10 Ⓕ Ⓖ Ⓗ Ⓙ Ⓚ	19 Ⓐ Ⓑ Ⓒ Ⓓ Ⓔ	28 Ⓕ Ⓖ Ⓗ Ⓙ Ⓚ
2 Ⓕ Ⓖ Ⓗ Ⓙ Ⓚ	11 Ⓐ Ⓑ Ⓒ Ⓓ Ⓔ	20 Ⓕ Ⓖ Ⓗ Ⓙ Ⓚ	29 Ⓐ Ⓑ Ⓒ Ⓓ Ⓔ
3 Ⓐ Ⓑ Ⓒ Ⓓ Ⓔ	12 Ⓕ Ⓖ Ⓗ Ⓙ Ⓚ	21 Ⓐ Ⓑ Ⓒ Ⓓ Ⓔ	30 Ⓕ Ⓖ Ⓗ Ⓙ Ⓚ
4 Ⓕ Ⓖ Ⓗ Ⓙ Ⓚ	13 Ⓐ Ⓑ Ⓒ Ⓓ Ⓔ	22 Ⓕ Ⓖ Ⓗ Ⓙ Ⓚ	31 Ⓐ Ⓑ Ⓒ Ⓓ Ⓔ
5 Ⓐ Ⓑ Ⓒ Ⓓ Ⓔ	14 Ⓕ Ⓖ Ⓗ Ⓙ Ⓚ	23 Ⓐ Ⓑ Ⓒ Ⓓ Ⓔ	32 Ⓕ Ⓖ Ⓗ Ⓙ Ⓚ
6 Ⓕ Ⓖ Ⓗ Ⓙ Ⓚ	15 Ⓐ Ⓑ Ⓒ Ⓓ Ⓔ	24 Ⓕ Ⓖ Ⓗ Ⓙ Ⓚ	33 Ⓐ Ⓑ Ⓒ Ⓓ Ⓔ
7 Ⓐ Ⓑ Ⓒ Ⓓ Ⓔ	16 Ⓕ Ⓖ Ⓗ Ⓙ Ⓚ	25 Ⓐ Ⓑ Ⓒ Ⓓ Ⓔ	34 Ⓕ Ⓖ Ⓗ Ⓙ Ⓚ
8 Ⓕ Ⓖ Ⓗ Ⓙ Ⓚ	17 Ⓐ Ⓑ Ⓒ Ⓓ Ⓔ	26 Ⓕ Ⓖ Ⓗ Ⓙ Ⓚ	35 Ⓐ Ⓑ Ⓒ Ⓓ Ⓔ
9 Ⓐ Ⓑ Ⓒ Ⓓ Ⓔ	18 Ⓕ Ⓖ Ⓗ Ⓙ Ⓚ	27 Ⓐ Ⓑ Ⓒ Ⓓ Ⓔ	36 Ⓕ Ⓖ Ⓗ Ⓙ Ⓚ

STEP TWO: SKILLS REVIEW

Day Two PSAE

STEP TWO: SKILLS REVIEW

AMERICA'S #1 STANDARDS-BASED SCHOOL IMPROVEMENT PROGRAM

Cambridge Course Concept Outline
STEP TWO

I. DAY TWO PSAE STEP TWO PROGRESS REPORTS (p. 33)

    A. DAY TWO PSAE STEP TWO STUDENT PROGRESS REPORT—SCIENCE SKILLS REVIEW (p. 33)

    B. DAY TWO PSAE STEP TWO INSTRUCTOR PROGRESS REPORT—SCIENCE SKILLS REVIEW (p. 35)

    C. DAY TWO PSAE STEP TWO STUDENT PROGRESS REPORT—MATHEMATICS SKILLS REVIEW (p. 37)

    D. DAY TWO PSAE STEP TWO INSTRUCTOR PROGRESS REPORT—MATHEMATICS SKILLS REVIEW (p. 39)

    E. DAY TWO PSAE STEP TWO STUDENT PROGRESS REPORT—READING SKILLS REVIEW (p. 41)

    F. DAY TWO PSAE STEP TWO INSTRUCTOR PROGRESS REPORT—READING SKILLS REVIEW (p. 43)

DAY TWO PSAE
STEP TWO PROGRESS REPORT
(Student Copy)

The Step Two Progress Reports are designed to help you monitor your Science Skills Review progress. The Science Skills Review exercises are located in the *Cambridge ACT • PLAN • EXPLORE Victory Student Textbook, 7th Edition.*

DIRECTIONS: Complete the assigned problems corresponding to each Science Skills Review lesson, correct your answers, and record both the number and percentage of problems that you answered correctly. Identify the date on which you completed each exercise. Your teacher will instruct you on whether additional review problems are necessary.

Transfer this information to the Instructor Copy, and then give that report to your instructor.

Note: The following form refers to the *Cambridge ACT • PLAN • EXPLORE Victory Student Textbook, 7th Edition.* Similar exercises may be found in the *Cambridge ACT • PLAN • EXPLORE Science Reasoning Victory Student Textbook* or in the *Cambridge Skills Review Textbook,* but the exercises, names, and problem counts may vary.

Name _____ Student ID _____ Date _____

SCIENCE SKILLS REVIEW
(Student Copy)

Exercise	Total # Possible	Assigned	# Correct	% Correct	Date Completed	Problem #s to Review
1. Basics of Experimental Design	7					
2. Data Organization in Controlled Experiments	9					
3. Presentation of Conflicting Viewpoints	4					
4. Science Reasoning Passages	24					

DAY TWO PSAE
STEP TWO PROGRESS REPORT
(Instructor Copy)

The Step Two Progress Reports are designed to help you monitor your Science Skills Review progress. The Science Skills Review exercises are located in the *Cambridge ACT • PLAN • EXPLORE Victory Student Textbook, 7th Edition.*

DIRECTIONS: Transfer the information from your Student Copy to the Instructor Copy below. Leave the last three bolded columns blank. Your instructor will use them to evaluate your progress. When finished, give this report to your instructor.

Note: The following form refers to the *Cambridge ACT • PLAN • EXPLORE Victory Student Textbook, 7th Edition.* Similar exercises may be found in the *Cambridge ACT • PLAN • EXPLORE Science Reasoning Victory Student Textbook* or in the *Cambridge Skills Review Textbook*, but the exercises, names, and problem counts may vary.

Student Name _____ Student ID _____ Date _____

SCIENCE SKILLS REVIEW
(Instructor Copy)

Exercise	Total # Possible	Total # Assigned	# Correct	% Correct	Date Completed	Problem #s to Review	Instructor Skill Evaluation (Check One Per Exercise) Mastered	Partially Mastered	Not Mastered
1. Basics of Experimental Design	7								
2. Data Organization in Controlled Experiments	9								
3. Presentation of Conflicting Viewpoints	4								
4. Science Reasoning Passages	24								

DAY TWO PSAE
STEP TWO PROGRESS REPORT
(Student Copy)

The Step Two Progress Reports are designed to help you monitor your Math Skills Review progress. The Math Skills Review exercises are located in the *Cambridge ACT • PLAN • EXPLORE Victory Student Textbook, 7th Edition.*

DIRECTIONS: Complete the assigned problems corresponding to each Math Skills Review lesson, correct your answers, and record both the number and percentage of problems that you answered correctly. Identify the date on which you completed each exercise. Your teacher will instruct you on whether additional review problems are necessary.

Transfer this information to the Instructor Copy, and then give that report to your instructor.

Note: The following form refers to the *Cambridge ACT • PLAN • EXPLORE Victory Student Textbook, 7th Edition.* Similar exercises may be found in the *Cambridge ACT • PLAN • EXPLORE Mathematics Victory Student Textbook* or in the *Cambridge Skills Review Textbook*, but the exercises, names, and problem counts may vary.

Name _____ Student ID _____ Date _____

MATHEMATICS SKILLS REVIEW
(Student Copy)

Exercise	Total # Possible	Assigned	# Correct	% Correct	Date Completed	Problem #s to Review
1. Whole Numbers	64					
2. Fractions	71					
3. Decimals	68					
4. Percents	128					
5. Negative Numbers	62					
6. Mean, Median, and Mode	47					
7. Ratios and Proportions	50					
8. Exponents and Radicals	70					
9. Algebraic Operations	103					
10. Equations and Inequalities	94					
11. Geometry	135-					
12. Coordinate Geometry	27					
13. Problem-Solving	44					

DAY TWO PSAE
STEP TWO PROGRESS REPORT
(Instructor Copy)

The Step Two Progress Reports are designed to help you monitor your Math Skills Review progress. The Math Skills Review exercises are located in the *Cambridge ACT • PLAN • EXPLORE Victory Student Textbook, 7th Edition.*

DIRECTIONS: Transfer the information from your Student Copy to the Instructor Copy below. Leave the last three bolded columns blank. Your instructor will use them to evaluate your progress. When finished, give this report to your instructor.

Note: The following form refers to the *Cambridge ACT • PLAN • EXPLORE Victory Student Textbook, 7th Edition.* Similar exercises may be found in the *Cambridge ACT • PLAN • EXPLORE Mathematics Victory Student Textbook* or in the *Cambridge Skills Review Textbook,* but the exercises, names, and problem counts may vary.

Student Name _____ Student ID _____ Date _____

MATHEMATICS SKILLS REVIEW
(Instructor Copy)

Exercise	Total # Possible	Assigned	# Correct	% Correct	Date Completed	Problem #s to Review	Mastered	Partially Mastered	Not Mastered
1. Whole Numbers	64								
2. Fractions	71								
3. Decimals	68								
4. Percents	128								
5. Negative Numbers	62								
6. Mean, Median, and Mode	47								
7. Ratios and Proportions	50								
8. Exponents and Radicals	70								
9. Algebraic Operations	103								
10. Equations and Inequalities	94								
11. Geometry	135-								
12. Coordinate Geometry	27								
13. Problem-Solving	44								

Instructor Skill Evaluation (Check One Per Exercise) applies to the Mastered / Partially Mastered / Not Mastered columns.

DAY TWO PSAE
STEP TWO PROGRESS REPORT
(Student Copy)

The Step Two Progress Reports are designed to help you monitor your Reading Skills Review progress. The Reading Skills Review exercises are located in the *Cambridge ACT • PLAN • EXPLORE Victory Student Textbook, 7th Edition.*

DIRECTIONS: Complete the assigned problems corresponding to each Reading Skills Review lesson, correct your answers, and record both the number and percentage of problems that you answered correctly. Identify the date on which you completed each exercise. Your teacher will instruct you on whether additional review problems are necessary.

Transfer this information to the Instructor Copy, and then give that report to your instructor.

Note: The following form refers to the *Cambridge ACT • PLAN • EXPLORE Victory Student Textbook, 7th Edition.* Similar exercises may be found in the *Cambridge ACT • PLAN • EXPLORE Reading Victory Student Textbook* or in the *Cambridge Skills Review Textbook,* but the exercises, names, and problem counts may vary.

Name _____ Student ID _____ Date _____

READING SKILLS REVIEW
(Student Copy)

Exercise	Total # Possible	Assigned	# Correct	% Correct	Date Completed	Problem #s to Review
1. Careful Reading of English Question Stems	19					
2. Careful Reading of Math Question Stems	20					
3. Careful Reading of Reading Question Stems	27					
4. Careful Reading of Science Question Stems	16					
5. Coding of Question Stems	43					
6. Vocabulary-in-Context: Reading Passages	10					
7. Vocabulary-in-Context: Sentence Completions	32					

DAY TWO PSAE
STEP TWO PROGRESS REPORT
(Instructor Copy)

The Step Two Progress Reports are designed to help you monitor your Reading Skills Review progress. The Reading Skills Review exercises are located in the *Cambridge ACT • PLAN • EXPLORE Victory Student Textbook, 7th Edition.*

DIRECTIONS: Transfer the information from your Student Copy to the Instructor Copy below. Leave the last three bolded columns blank. Your instructor will use them to evaluate your progress. When finished, give this report to your instructor.

Note: The following form refers to the *Cambridge ACT • PLAN • EXPLORE Victory Student Textbook, 7th Edition.* Similar exercises may be found in the *Cambridge ACT • PLAN • EXPLORE Reading Victory Student Textbook* or in the *Cambridge Skills Review Textbook*, but the exercises, names, and problem counts may vary.

Student Name _____ Student ID _____ Date _____

READING SKILLS REVIEW
(Instructor Copy)

	Total #						Instructor Skill Evaluation (Check One Per Exercise)		
Exercise	*Possible*	*Assigned*	*# Correct*	*% Correct*	*Date Completed*	*Problem #s to Review*	*Mastered*	*Partially Mastered*	*Not Mastered*
1. Careful Reading of English Question Stems	19								
2. Careful Reading of Math Question Stems	20								
3. Careful Reading of Reading Question Stems	27								
4. Careful Reading of Science Question Stems	16								
5. Coding of Question Stems	43								
6. Vocabulary-in-Context: Reading Passages	10								
7. Vocabulary-in-Context: Sentence Completions	32								

STEP THREE: PROBLEM-SOLVING, CONCEPTS, AND STRATEGIES

Day Two PSAE

STEP THREE: PROBLEM-SOLVING, CONCEPTS, AND STRATEGIES

AMERICA'S #1 STANDARDS-BASED SCHOOL IMPROVEMENT PROGRAM

Cambridge Course Concept Outline
STEP THREE

II. SECTION ONE—READING FOR INFORMATION REVIEW (p. 123)

A. OVERVIEW OF THE READING FOR INFORMATION LESSON

B. INTRODUCTION TO THE READING FOR INFORMATION TEST

C. FORMAT OF THE READING FOR INFORMATION TEST

D. FIVE LEVELS OF QUESTION DIFFICULTY

1. LEVEL 3 QUESTIONS
2. LEVEL 4 QUESTIONS
3. LEVEL 5 QUESTIONS
4. LEVEL 6 QUESTIONS
5. LEVEL 7 QUESTIONS

E. TEST-TAKING STRATEGIES

1. READ THROUGH ENTIRE PASSAGE
2. DON'T TRY TO MEMORIZE DETAILS
3. MARK IMPORTANT POINTS
4. PAY ATTENTION TO UNDERLYING CONCERNS
5. ELIMINATE CHOICES AND GUESS

F. EIGHT MAJOR CATEGORIES OF QUESTIONS

1. MAIN IDEA
2. DETAILS
3. VOCABULARY
4. COMPARATIVE RELATIONSHIPS
5. CAUSE/EFFECT
6. SEQUENCE
7. GENERALIZATIONS
8. AUTHOR'S VOICE

G. READING FOR INFORMATION WALK-THROUGH
(Review Questions #1-10, p. 123)

1. PASSAGE I (p. 123)
   a. CAUSE/EFFECT (Review Questions #1-2, p. 124)
   b. DETAILS (Review Question #3, p. 124)
   c. COMPARATIVE RELATIONSHIPS (Review Question #4, p. 124)
   d. AUTHOR'S VOICE (Review Question #5, p. 124)
2. PASSAGE II (p. 125)
   a. SEQUENCE (Review Question #6, p. 125)
   b. DETAILS (Review Questions #7-8, p. 125)
3. PASSAGE III (p. 126)
   a. SEQUENCE (Review Question #9, p. 127)
   b. VOCABULARY (Review Question #10, p. 127)
   c. DETAILS (Review Questions #11-12, p. 127)

DAY TWO PSAE
STEP THREE PROGRESS REPORT
(Student Copy)

The Step Three Progress Reports are designed to help you monitor your Day Two PSAE Step Three progress.

DIRECTIONS: Complete the assigned problems corresponding to each lesson for Step Three, correct your answers, and record both the number and percentage of problems that you answered correctly. Identify the date on which you completed each exercise. Your teacher will instruct you on whether additional review problems are necessary.

Transfer this information to the Instructor Copy, and then give that report to your instructor.

Name _____ Student ID _____ Date _____

ISBE-DEVELOPED SCIENCE
(Student Copy)

Section	Total # Possible	Assigned	# Correct	% Correct	Date Completed	Problem #s to Review
1. Section One—Science Review (p. 71)	33					
2. Section Two—Science Problem-Solving (p. 77)	10					
3. Section Three—Science Quiz 1 (p. 80)	13					
4. Section Three—Science Quiz 2 (p. 83)	13					
5. Section Three—Science Quiz 3 (p. 86)	14					

DAY TWO PSAE
STEP THREE PROGRESS REPORT
(Instructor Copy)

The Step Three Progress Reports are designed to help you monitor your Day Two PSAE Step Three progress.

DIRECTIONS: Transfer the information from your Student Copy to the Instructor Copy below. Leave the last three bolded columns blank. Your instructor will use them to evaluate your progress. When finished, give this report to your instructor.

Student Name _____ Student ID _____ Date _____

ISBE-DEVELOPED SCIENCE
(Instructor Copy)

Section	Total #						Instructor Skill Evaluation (Check One Per Section)		
	Possible	Assigned	# Correct	% Correct	Date Completed	Problem #s to Review	Mastered	Partially Mastered	Not Mastered
1. Section One—Science Review (p. 71)	33								
2. Section Two—Science Problem-Solving (p. 77)	10								
3. Section Three—Science Quiz 1 (p. 80)	13								
4. Section Three—Science Quiz 2 (p. 83)	13								
5. Section Three—Science Quiz 3 (p. 86)	14								

DAY TWO PSAE
STEP THREE PROGRESS REPORT
(Student Copy)

The Step Three Progress Reports are designed to help you monitor your Day Two PSAE Step Three progress.

DIRECTIONS: Complete the assigned problems corresponding to each lesson for Step Three, correct your answers, and record both the number and percentage of problems that you answered correctly. Identify the date on which you completed each exercise. Your teacher will instruct you on whether additional review problems are necessary.

Transfer this information to the Instructor Copy, and then give that report to your instructor.

Name _____ Student ID _____ Date _____

APPLIED MATHEMATICS
(Student Copy)

Section	Total # Possible	Assigned	# Correct	% Correct	Date Completed	Problem #s to Review
1. Section One—Applied Mathematics Review (p. 96)	60					
2. Section Two—Applied Mathematics Problem-Solving (p. 106)	10					
3. Section Three—Applied Mathematics Quiz 1 (p. 109)	10					
4. Section Three—Applied Mathematics Quiz 2 (p. 111)	10					
5. Section Three—Applied Mathematics Quiz 3 (p. 113)	11					

DAY TWO PSAE
STEP THREE PROGRESS REPORT
(Instructor Copy)

The Step Three Progress Reports are designed to help you monitor your Day Two PSAE Step Three progress.

DIRECTIONS: Transfer the information from your Student Copy to the Instructor Copy below. Leave the last three bolded columns blank. Your instructor will use them to evaluate your progress. When finished, give this report to your instructor.

Student Name _____ Student ID _____ Date _____

APPLIED MATHEMATICS
(Instructor Copy)

Section	Total # Possible	Assigned	# Correct	% Correct	Date Completed	Problem #s to Review	Instructor Skill Evaluation (Check One Per Section) Mastered	Partially Mastered	Not Mastered
1. Section One—Applied Mathematics Review (p. 96)	60								
2. Section Two—Applied Mathematics Problem-Solving (p. 106)	10								
3. Section Three—Applied Mathematics Quiz 1 (p. 109)	10								
4. Section Three—Applied Mathematics Quiz 2 (p. 111)	10								
5. Section Three—Applied Mathematics Quiz 3 (p. 113)	11								

DAY TWO PSAE
STEP THREE PROGRESS REPORT
(Student Copy)

The Step Three Progress Reports are designed to help you monitor your Day Two PSAE Step Three progress.

DIRECTIONS: Complete the assigned problems corresponding to each lesson for Step Three, correct your answers, and record both the number and percentage of problems that you answered correctly. Identify the date on which you completed each exercise. Your teacher will instruct you on whether additional review problems are necessary.

Transfer this information to the Instructor Copy, and then give that report to your instructor.

Name _____ Student ID _____ Date _____

READING FOR INFORMATION
(Student Copy)

Section	Total # Possible	Assigned	# Correct	% Correct	Date Completed	Problem #s to Review
1. Section One—Reading for Information Review (p. 123)	12					
2. Section Two—Reading for Information Problem-Solving (p. 129)	8					
3. Section Three—Reading for Information Quiz 1 (p. 133)	12					
4. Section Three—Reading for Information Quiz 2 (p. 139)	10					
5. Section Three—Reading for Information Quiz 3 (p. 144)	11					

DAY TWO PSAE
STEP THREE PROGRESS REPORT
(Instructor Copy)

The Step Three Progress Reports are designed to help you monitor your Day Two PSAE Step Three progress.

DIRECTIONS: Transfer the information from your Student Copy to the Instructor Copy below. Leave the last three bolded columns blank. Your instructor will use them to evaluate your progress. When finished, give this report to your instructor.

Student Name _____ Student ID _____ Date _____

READING FOR INFORMATION
(Instructor Copy)

Section	Total #		# Correct	% Correct	Date Completed	Problem #s to Review	Instructor Skill Evaluation (Check One Per Section)		
	Possible	*Assigned*					*Mastered*	*Partially Mastered*	*Not Mastered*
1. Section One—Reading for Information Review (p. 123)	12								
2. Section Two—Reading for Information Problem-Solving (p. 129)	8								
3. Section Three—Reading for Information Quiz 1 (p. 133)	12								
4. Section Three—Reading for Information Quiz 2 (p. 139)	10								
5. Section Three—Reading for Information Quiz 3 (p. 144)	11								

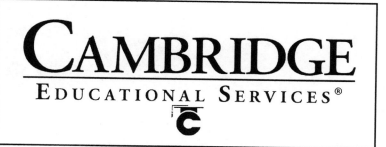

Day Two PSAE

ISBE-DEVELOPED SCIENCE

AMERICA'S #1 STANDARDS-BASED SCHOOL IMPROVEMENT PROGRAM

Cambridge Course Concept Outline
STEP THREE

I. SECTION ONE—ISBE-DEVELOPED SCIENCE REVIEW (p. 71)

A. OVERVIEW OF THE ISBE-DEVELOPED SCIENCE LESSON

B. INTRODUCTION TO THE ISBE-DEVELOPED SCIENCE TEST

C. FORMAT OF THE ISBE-DEVELOPED SCIENCE TEST

D. TEST-TAKING STRATEGIES

1. **READ THE QUESTION CAREFULLY** (Review Question #1, p. 71)
2. **CONSIDER ALL THE ANSWER CHOICES** (Review Question #2, p. 71)
3. **CAREFULLY STUDY ANY ADDITIONAL INFORMATION** (Review Question #3, p. 71)
4. **ELIMINATE AS MANY CHOICES AS POSSIBLE** (Review Question #4, p. 72)
5. **USE ALL OF YOUR KNOWLEDGE** (Review Question #5, p. 72)

E. SEVEN MAJOR CATEGORIES OF QUESTIONS

1. **BIOLOGY** (Review Questions #6-10, p. 72)
2. **CHEMISTRY** (Review Questions #11-13, p. 72)
3. **PHYSICS** (Review Questions #14-19, p. 73)
4. **EARTH** (Review Questions #20-23, p. 74)
5. **SPACE** (Review Questions #24-26, p. 74)
6. **ECOLOGY** (Review Questions #27-29, p. 74)
7. **SOCIETY** (Review Questions #30-33, p. 74)

II. SECTION TWO—ISBE-DEVELOPED SCIENCE PROBLEM-SOLVING (p. 77)

III. SECTION THREE—ISBE-DEVELOPED SCIENCE QUIZZES (p. 80)

A. QUIZ I (p. 80)

B. QUIZ II (p. 83)

C. QUIZ III (p. 86)

IV. STRATEGY SUMMARY SHEET—ISBE-DEVELOPED SCIENCE (p. 88)

SECTION ONE—ISBE-DEVELOPED SCIENCE REVIEW

DIRECTIONS: The questions in this section accompany the in-class review of the Science concepts and skills tested by the PSAE ISBE-Developed Science test. You will work through the questions with your instructor in class. Each data summary or short prompt is followed by one multiple-choice question. Choose the best answer. Answers are on page 213.

1. The burning of fuel results in the production of

   A. Oxygen
   B. Hydrogen
   C. Water
   D. Alcohol

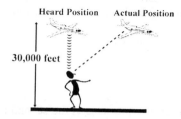

2. The diagram above compares the position of the plane as judged by the observer. Based upon the sound made by the plane compared with the actual position of the plane, which of the following best explains this phenomenon?

   A. The plane is flying faster than the speed of sound.
   B. The speed of light is much greater than the speed of sound.
   C. The observer hears the plane only when it is directly overhead.
   D. The "Heard Position" plane depends upon the volume of the sound.

SUMMER

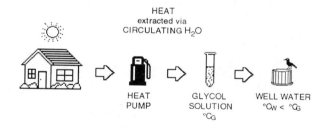

WINTER

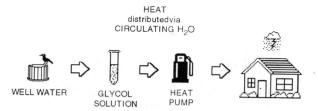

3. The above diagram illustrates a household climate control system that uses geothermal energy. During the summer, heat is extracted from the house by the circulating water, transferred by the heat pump to the glycol solution, and dissipated into the relatively cooler well water. During the winter, the glycol solution absorbs heat from the well water, which is then transferred by the heat pump to the circulating water for distribution to the house. Which of the following best explains why the system would probably not work as well for heating purposes in an area with mild winters as in an area with fairly cold winter temperatures?

   A. The water in the bored well would likely freeze in a region with severe winters.
   B. The temperature differential between the ground water and the air would be too small.
   C. Frictional forces inside the heat pump would cause the build-up of excess heat energy.
   D. The glycol solution would remain in a liquid state in all relevant temperatures.

4. In the normal human circulatory system, the mean blood pressure is lowest in which of the following?

A. Aorta
B. Arteries
C. Arterioles
D. Capillaries

5. Sound is a longitudinal wave that must be propagated through a medium. Consequently, sound cannot travel in a vacuum. Through which of the following does sound travel most rapidly?

A. Air
B. Cork
C. Steel
D. Water

6. In enclosed automobile repair shops where technicians work on running engines, hoses connect the automobile exhaust pipes to the outside air. Which of the following best explains why the hoses are used?

A. To bring in oxygen that is needed to ensure that the car engine continues to run
B. To carry carbon monoxide and other hazardous by-products of the internal combustion engine
C. To channel sound waves to the outside thus reducing the noise level in the repair shop
D. To provide a ground for the electrical systems of the engines to minimize the risk of fire

7. Life processes that take place in most animals include all of the following EXCEPT:

A. Using energy for metabolism
B. Elimination of water and waste
C. Reproduction
D. Giving off oxygen

8. The correct sequence of organs in the human digestive structure is:

A. small intestine, esophagus, stomach, large intestine.
B. stomach, spleen, liver, large intestine.
C. esophagus, stomach, large intestine, small intestine.
D. esophagus, stomach, small intestine, large intestine.

9. Diets that are low in carbohydrates are very popular. To cut down on carbohydrates, which of the following foods should be avoided?

A. Fish
B. Poultry
C. Breads
D. Cheese

10. If a doctor describes a patient as dehydrated, the patient:

A. has a need for hydrogen.
B. needs insulin.
C. has lost a great deal of water.
D. has just been given intravenous fluids.

11. Absolute zero is the lowest possible temperature. In terms of the Celsius scale, this temperature is:

A. $0°$ C.
B. $-273°$ C.
C. $-459°$ C.
D. $-820°$ C.

12. Which of the following is the second most abundant molecule in the air surrounding the Earth?

A. Oxygen
B. Nitrogen
C. Carbon dioxide
D. Helium

13. Atoms consist of one or more positively charged particles called protons, negatively charged particles called electrons, and various numbers of neutral particles called neutrons. Which of the following is true of a positively charged ion?

A. It has more protons than electrons.
B. It has an equal number of protons and electrons.
C. It has more electrons than protons.
D. It has no electrons.

14. As a star runs out of nuclear fuel, it eventually dies, leaving behind one of several possible objects such as a white dwarf star, a red giant star, or a black hole. Which of the following characteristics of the star is the most important factor in determining what kind of object will be left at the end of the star's life cycle?

   A. Age
   B. Location
   C. Mass
   D. Color

15. A team of scientists at the XYZ Research Center announced that they had produced heat by a process called cold fusion in a laboratory experiment. They described the procedures of the experiment in great detail. Several other teams of scientists at universities as well as government and other private labs tried the experiment but failed to get the same result. Which of the following conclusions can most reliably be drawn?

   A. Scientific research done at universities and government labs is less reliable than that done in private labs.
   B. The original cold fusion experiment was successful, but the results could only be achieved under the unique conditions of the XYZ lab.
   C. The team at XYZ Research Center did not mention several top-secret devices needed to achieve the positive experimental outcome.
   D. The team at XYZ Research Center did not accurately record their observations of the result of the experiment.

16. Sound travels fastest when it moves through which of the following mediums?

   A. A solid
   B. A liquid
   C. A gas
   D. A vacuum

17. In the diagram above, a rocket has just left the Earth. The rocket's thrusters battle to overcome the gravitational force between the rocket and the Earth. The force from the thrusters is a(n):

   A. weak force.
   B. electromagnetic force.
   C. strong force.
   D. nuclear force.

18. Shooting stars are not really stars at all. These bright flashes of moving light are caused by small bits of interplanetary rock and debris (called meteoroids) traveling at thousands of miles per hour that are entering the Earth's upper atmosphere. Which of the following BEST explains why the meteoroids give off a bright light?

   A. Friction causes the meteoroids to burn up.
   B. The rock and debris are magnetized.
   C. Shooting or falling stars are radioactive.
   D. The meteoroids reflect light from the moon.

19. A construction worker is trying to move a heavy boulder using a steel bar as shown in the diagram above. If the worker isn't strong enough, which of the following is likely to be most effective in moving the boulder?

   A. A shorter steel bar
   B. A longer steel bar
   C. A shorter aluminum bar
   D. A heavier concrete block

20. The San Andreas fault is associated most frequently with:

    A. tidal waves in Japan.
    B. geyser actions in Oregon.
    C. volcanoes in Washington.
    D. earthquakes in California.

21. The correct sequence for the geological time scale is:

    A. Precambrian, Paleozoic, Mesozoic, Cenozoic.
    B. Mesozoic, Precambrian, Paleozoic, Cenozoic.
    C. Precambrian, Mesozoic, Cenozoic, Paleozoic.
    D. Mesozoic, Precambrian, Cenozoic, Paleozoic.

22. Which of the following statements best characterizes the Earth's continents?

    A. The continents are now believed to be moving very slowly.
    B. The continents are now believed to have been immobile since their formation.
    C. The continents cover most of the Earth's surface.
    D. The movements of the continents coincide with the tidal changes.

23. High and low tides are primarily caused by:

    A. the orbit of the sun.
    B. the orbit of Earth's closest planet, Mars.
    C. the orbit of the moon.
    D. the forces of the Milky Way.

24. The planet that revolves around the sun in an orbit between Venus and Mars is:

    A. Jupiter.
    B. Saturn.
    C. Earth.
    D. Mercury.

25. Stars are composed mainly of:

    A. hydrogen and helium.
    B. hydrogen and oxygen.
    C. oxygen and nitrogen.
    D. helium and neon.

26. As a star runs out of nuclear fuel, it eventually dies, leaving behind one of several possible objects. Which of the following is <u>not</u> a star that is in the last stage of its life cycle?

    A. White dwarfs
    B. Red giants
    C. Black holes
    D. Pale ogres

27. The best illustration of a food chain is:

    A. algae-larval insect-fish-man.
    B. fish-larval insect-algae-man.
    C. larval insect-algae-fish-man.
    D. algae-fish-larval insect-man.

28. The word "symbiotic" most nearly means:

    A. mutually beneficial.
    B. dependent on light.
    C. naturally occurring.
    D. not threatening.

29. Some insect pests that were once easily controlled by various chemical sprays are now resistant to those chemicals, making them more difficult to control. Which of the following BEST explains why the insects are now resistant to the chemicals?

    A. Mutation
    B. Respiration
    C. Fertilization
    D. Transportation

30. Cyclic changes are predictable changes in our environment. If we collected data on the time between the instances of each change listed below, which one would be least likely to appear as cyclic?

    A. Earthquakes
    B. Change of seasons
    C. Tides
    D. Eclipses

31. The sign above appears in an automobile repair shop. Which of the following best explains the shop's policy?

    A. A car's engine cannot operate in a closed garage.

    B. The exhaust from a car's engine contains poisonous carbon monoxide.

    C. Opening the outer doors cools the car's engine.

    D. Outside air circulating through the space makes the engine run less efficiently.

32. Research indicates that cigarette smoking results in which of the following conditions?

    A. Swollen glands
    B. Pulmonary stress
    C. Hepatitis
    D. Dermatitis

33. Human interferon can be used to fight viral infections. This means that interferon may be helpful in curing:

    A. diseases that are responsible for deformities.

    B. diseases that are genetic in origin.

    C. problems related to psychological stress.

    D. the common cold.

 STEP THREE

NOTES AND STRATEGIES

SECTION TWO—ISBE-DEVELOPED SCIENCE PROBLEM-SOLVING

DIRECTIONS: This section contains Science problems for in-class problem-solving with your instructor. Each data summary or short prompt is followed by one multiple-choice question. Choose the best answer. Answers are on page 213.

1. Bears, wolves, squirrels, and fir and spruce trees are usually found in which of the following biomes?

   A. Grasslands
   B. Deserts
   C. Taigas
   D. Veldts

2. Diets high in saturated fat and cholesterol have been linked to heart disease and a diet high in fat to some cancers. To cut down on saturated fats and cholesterol, which of the following foods should be avoided?

   A. Fish
   B   Poultry
   C. Cheese
   D. Spaghetti

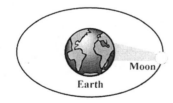

Sun   Earth

3. The illustration above depicts which one of the following?

   A. Solar eclipse
   B. Lunar eclipse
   C. Solar flare
   D. Planetary eclipse

4. The process by which rocks are broken down into smaller fragments by the atmosphere and other factors in the environment is called

   A. Erosion
   B. Sorting
   C. Glaciation
   D. Weathering

---

1. Identical fossil species of terrestrial plants and animals are found in Africa, South Africa, India, and Australia.

2. The Cape Mountains of South Africa are the same type of folded mountains, made up of the same type rocks as the mountains south of Buenos Aires in South America.

3. The rock on the crests of the mid-oceanic ridges is younger than the rock on either side of the crest.

---

5. The three observations above most strongly support which of the following conclusions?

   A. The ocean floor consists of rock types that are older than those that comprise the exposed surface of the land.
   B. The Earth was formed by the cooling and shrinking of an originally molten mass.
   C. At one time, all of the land on the surface of the Earth was a single continent that later split apart.
   D. Species that are found to be identical in remote locations probably arrived there by migration.

6. A small object is placed into a container filled with water. The amount of water that is displaced from the container and overflows is a function of the

   A. Weight of the object
   B. Volume of the object
   C. Shape of the object
   D. Chemical composition of the object

7. Which of the following types of energy is transmitted by electromagnetic waves?

   A. Light
   B. Sound
   C. Heat
   D. Work

8. Early Monday morning, 15 people arrived at the emergency room of Mercy Hospital between 4:00 am and 5:00 am all complaining of stomach cramps and nausea. Which of the following questions would be most appropriate to ask the patients to determine whether or not they had contracted food poisoning?

   A. The city, state, and country where they were born
   B. Where and what they had eaten Sunday evening
   C. Where they live and for how long they've lived there
   D. Whether or not they have allergies to medications

9. In a particular area of the Northeastern United States, grass fires are most common during the months of February and March. Which of the following most likely explains this pattern?

   A. The growing season ends in the autumn in the region, so the grass is driest during those months.
   B. Thunderstorms accompanied by violent lightening usually occur during the winter months in the area.
   C. Temperatures in the region are higher during February and March than in the other months of the year.
   D. Snow blankets the ground during those months, trapping heat and causing fires to start.

10. At which of the points shown would the least amount of applied force be needed to move the weight?

    A. 1
    B. 2
    C. 3
    D. 4

NOTES AND STRATEGIES

SECTION THREE—ISBE-DEVELOPED SCIENCE QUIZZES

DIRECTIONS: This section contains three Science quizzes. Complete each quiz while being timed. Answers are on page 213.

QUIZ I (13 questions; 13 minutes)

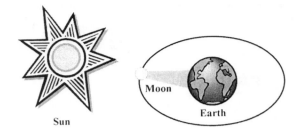

1. The noble gases include elements that have atoms with complete outer electron shells. Neon, argon, xenon are noble gases. Which of the following statements about argon is correct?

    A. Argon naturally occurs as a gas in several different colors.
    B. Argon does not ordinarily form compounds with other elements.
    C. Argon is found in liquid form as well as gaseous form.
    D. Argon exists in greater quantities than either neon or xenon.

2. Atoms consist of one or more positively charged particles called protons, negatively charged particles called electrons, and various numbers of neutral particles called neutrons. Which of the following is true of a negatively charged ion?

    A. The atom has more protons than neutrons.
    B. The atom has more electrons than protons.
    C. The atom has more neutrons than electrons.
    D. The atom has more neutrons than protons.

3. Which of the following processes is responsible for clothes drying on a line on a warm summer day?

    A. Condensation
    B. Sublimation
    C. Liquefaction
    D. Evaporation

4. The illustration above is an example of

    A. The phases of the moon
    B. The seasons of the year
    C. A lunar eclipse
    D. A solar eclipse

5. Which of the following is an unsafe laboratory practice?

    A. Turning off a Bunsen burner when it is not in use
    B. Utilizing a hood for handling toxic chemicals
    C. Diluting acid by slowly adding water
    D. Keeping the work area free of unneeded devices

6. A sample of one isotope of carbon, ^{14}C, is being studied. After a period of 28,000 years, it is determined that only $\frac{1}{32}$ of the sample of ^{14}C remains. What is the approximate half-life, in years, of ^{14}C?

    A. 4,200
    B. 5,600
    C. 7,000
    D. 14,000

7. Stone crabs are harvested for food on eastern shores of Florida. The crabs are captured; the large claw is pulled off; and the crabs are returned to the water where they continue to thrive and produce a new claw for the next year's harvest. The process by which the crabs produce a new claw each year is called

    A. Cloning
    B. Regeneration
    C. Pollination
    D. Reproduction

8. Which of the following best describes an ecological association in which one organism benefits from living on or within a host and which has an overall negative effect on the host?

  A. Predation
  B. Symbiosis
  C. Parasitism
  D. Mutualism

9. Food chains end with

  A. Producers
  B. Autotrophs
  C. Decomposers
  D. Primary Consumers

10. The main reservoir of carbon for the carbon cycle is which of the following?

  A. Hydrocarbons contained in coal and oil
  B. Calcium carbonate contained in limestone
  C. Carbon contained in diamonds
  D. Carbon dioxide in air and dissolved in water

11. Which of the following properties involves the transfer of energy by the collision of molecules?

  A. Radiation
  B. Convection
  C. Conduction
  D. Insulation

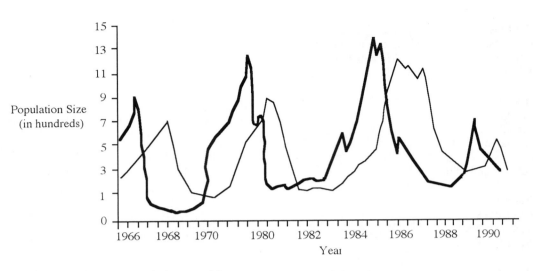

12. The graph above shows the population trend in a predator-prey system. Which of the following statements is most likely true?

    A. The bold line represents the predator population, the thin line the prey.
    B. A decrease in predator population is followed four years later by an increase in prey population.
    C. Several years after an increase in prey population, there is a parallel rise in predator population.
    D. There is no correlation between predator and prey populations.

13. The function of water in photosynthesis is to

    A. Absorb light energy
    B. Combine with CO_2
    C. Contribute electrons
    D. Provide O_2

QUIZ II (13 questions; 13 minutes)

1. Bats are able to sense the presence of objects through echolocation by emitting extremely high-pitched sounds and using the echoes to determine the location, size, and shape of the objects. How does echolocation enable insect-eating bats to avoid competing with birds for food?

   A. Bats can fly faster than the insects they hunt because they are not affected by light.
   B. Bats can cover greater distances than birds in their search for food.
   C. Bats do not hunt when temperatures are cool because few insects are available.
   D. Bats are able to hunt for insects at night while birds hunt during the day.

2. Electricity flowing through a conductor meets with resistance that generates heat and results in a reduction of current as measured in amperes. Which of the following circuits will produce the greatest reduction of current in the form of heat?

   A.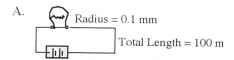
   Radius = 0.1 mm
   Total Length = 100 m

   B.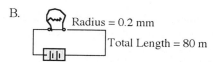
   Radius = 0.2 mm
   Total Length = 80 m

   C.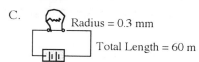
   Radius = 0.3 mm
   Total Length = 60 m

   D.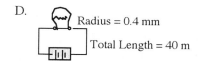
   Radius = 0.4 mm
   Total Length = 40 m

14.7 pounds per square inch

3. The diagram above represents a tall mountain. The atmospheric pressure at the bottom is 14.7 pounds per square inch.
   At the top of the mountain, the atmospheric pressure is

   A. Less because of a smaller amount of atmosphere pushing down
   B. Less because of the greater amount of atmosphere pushing down
   C. Greater since the ambient temperature is lower
   D. Greater since there is a greater proximity to the clouds

4. Inheritance of color in a certain plant is known to follow simple Mendelian rules. Green leaf color is dominant and yellow leaf color is recessive to green. If a homozygous green-leafed plant were mated with a homozygous yellow-leafed plant, what proportion of offspring (F_1 generation) would be expected to possess yellow leaves?

   A. 0%
   B. 25%
   C. 50%
   D. 100%

5. Enough Na_2SO_4 is dissolved in water at 40°C to saturate the solution. Which of the following statements is true?

   A. The boiling point of the resulting solution is higher than that of pure water.
   B. The freezing point of the resulting solution is higher than that of pure water.
   C. The boiling point of the resulting solution is lower than that of pure water.
   D. The freezing and boiling points of the resulting solution are the same as those of pure water.

6. In an experiment, a metal ball is dropped from a height of 10 meters. Which of the following graphs correctly describes the motion of the ball?

7. In the diagram below, a rocket has just left the Earth. The attractive force between the rocket and the Earth is

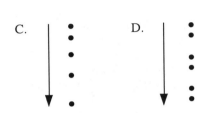

A. Magnetic
B. Electrical
C. Centripetal
D. Gravitational

8. A leaf from a green-and-white variegated coleus was placed in the sun for several hours; a similar leaf was stored in a darkened cabinet for several hours. Both leaves were then immersed in heated alcohol until colorless, patted dry with a paper towel, and then placed on a clean petri dish and flooded with Lugol's iodine, a chemical that turns blue-black in the presence of starch. The following table shows the results:

EXPOSED TO THE SUN		STORED IN THE DARK	
White Area of Leaf	Green Area of Leaf	White Area of Leaf	Green Area of Leaf
Brown	Brown	Brown	Blue-black

Which of the following best accounts for the result?

A. The chlorophyll in the green area of the leaf exposed to sunlight photosynthesized sugar, some of which was stored as starch.
B. Chlorophyll is deactivated when it comes into contact with Lugol's iodine.
C. The coleus leaf kept in the darkened cabinet contained an insignificant amount of chlorophyll.
D. The white area of both leafs contained chlorophyll in greater concentrations than the green areas.

9. A person who is susceptible to spontaneous hemorrhaging would most likely be treated with

A. Vitamin B
B. Vitamin C
C. Vitamin D
D. Vitamin K

10. A piece of lead at room temperature is a dull gray color. When the blade of a screwdriver scratches the lead, the resulting scar is bright and shiny. The shine quickly dulls due to the process of

   A. Reduction
   B. Oxidation
   C. Transformation
   D. Elimination

11. The head of a steel nail is brought into proximity with the south pole of a permanent magnet as shown in the diagram above. Which of the following statements is true?

   A. The nail is temporarily magnetized with the point as a north pole.
   B. The nail is temporarily magnetized with the point as a south pole.
   C. The nail is permanently magnetized with the head as the south pole and the point as the north pole.
   D. The nail is not affected by the magnetic properties of the permanent magnet.

12. Oxygen transported from the water to the bloodstream in the gills of fish occurs by a process called diffusion. Researchers have learned that the efficiency of oxygen extraction by the blood of fish in motion is higher than that of fish that are relatively still. Which of the following might explain the result?

   A. Diffusion of oxygen through a cell wall is a much more efficient process in a water environment than in air.
   B. The blood of the swimming fish circulates in the opposite direction of the water flowing through the gills.
   C. Multiple layers of cells separate the bloodstream of fish from the water in the gills containing the oxygen.
   D. A fish that is relatively still has less need for oxygen that one that is vigorously swimming.

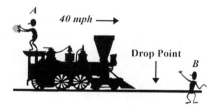

13. The diagram above shows an experiment in which Person A, standing on a moving train, is preparing to drop an iron ball weighing 20 pounds. Person B, standing on the ground, observes this event. Which of the following best describes what the two persons see when the ball is dropped?

   A. Person A sees the ball move forward from the time of release at the drop point while Person B sees the ball fall in a downward arc.
   B. Person A sees the ball fall straight to the ground from the drop point while Person B sees the ball fall in a downward arc.
   C. Person A sees the ball fall straight to the ground from the drop point while Person B sees the ball accelerate forward.
   D. Person A sees the ball strike the ground at the drop point, and Person B sees the ball strike the ground at the same point.

QUIZ III (14 questions; 13 minutes)

1. The Earth rotates on its axis, turning from west to east. This rotational movement accounts for

   A. Changes in the length of the day
   B. Long-term climatic variations
   C. The cyclical pattern of night and day
   D. Lower temperatures at the poles

2. Every few years off the western coasts of North and South America, an unusual warming trend occurs called "El Niño." Some scientists think that El Niño results from major volcanic eruptions that spew ash into the upper atmosphere, disrupting global weather patterns. Which of the following would be the best source for evidence that would be useful in testing this theory?

   A. Newspaper reports describing the devastating effects of weather patterns caused by El Niño
   B. Written records documenting volcanic eruptions coupled with temperature logs of weather stations
   C. Eyewitness accounts of people who live in areas with active volcanoes about their routine observations of volcanic sites
   D. Videotape footage created by geologists who filmed various volcanic eruptions

3. On the east coast of the United States, cities located on or near the ocean consistently record higher temperatures than cities farther inland on the same days during the winter. Which of the following best explains this phenomenon?

   A. Cities on the ocean receive sunlight for a greater number of hours during the day than cities farther inland.
   B. Sunlight striking the inland cities travels through more atmosphere than that striking the coastal cities.
   C. Water tends to cool more slowly than land so the ocean warms the coastal cities.
   D. The rotation of the Earth causes winds that move generally in a west-to-east direction.

4. Which of the following would be expected to have the most stable ecosystem?

   A. Ocean floor beneath Antarctic polar ice
   B. Pacific shore along California
   C. Subtropical forests of Africa
   D. Grasslands of Southwestern United States

5. Two guns, X and Y, aimed parallel to the ground, are fired over an extended level field. Which of the following is most important in determining which projectile, the one fired by X or the one fired by Y, goes further?

   A. The relative weights of the two projectiles
   B. The exact chemical composition of the two projectiles
   C. The initial velocities of each of the projectiles
   D. The ambient air temperature at the time of firing

6. An astronaut in a space station experiences "weightlessness." Which of the following best approximates the condition of weightlessness?

   A. An elevator in a skyscraper in freefall
   B. An airplane accelerating for take-off
   C. A speeding car that brakes suddenly
   D. A parachute drifting slowly to Earth

7. The Doppler effect accounts for the seeming change in the color of stars observed by an astronomer. If a star is moving away from the observer, the perceived frequency of the light will be lower and the color of the star will be shifted to the red end of the visible light spectrum. The Doppler effect predicts that a stationary observer who hears the whistle of an approaching train will detect

   A. A drop in pitch as the train passes and moves away
   B. A rise in pitch as the train passes and moves away
   C. An increase in volume as the train moves away
   D. A decrease in volume as the train passes by

8. In which of the following biomes is the technique of "slash-burn-cultivate-abandon" used for agriculture?

   A. Tundra
   B. Savannah
   C. Deciduous forest
   D. Tropical rain forest

Bacteria Growth in a Food Source

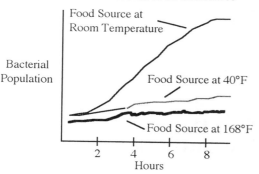

9. The diagram above most directly supports which of the following conclusions about safe food practices in a restaurant?

    A. It is important to store hot food at temperatures above 168°F and cold food at temperatures below 40°F.
    B. It is important to clean and disinfect all work surfaces with a commercial cleaner on a regular basis.
    C. It is unsafe to serve food to customers at temperatures above 40°F or below 168°F.
    D. Foods that are not consumed within two hours of preparation should be disposed of.

10. A flame test of a particular substance gives a persistent yellow color. Which of the following elements is most likely responsible?

    A. Sodium
    B. Hydrogen
    C. Oxygen
    D. Carbon

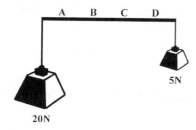

11. A massless plank supports two objects as shown above. The labeled areas divide the plank into sections of uniform length. At which point could the plank be lifted without the blocks causing rotation?

    A. A
    B. B
    C. C
    D. D

12. The following equation describes a system initially in equilibrium:

    $$2SO_2 + O_2 \leftrightarrow 2SO_3$$

    What will be the effect if the pressure in the system is increased?

    A. The concentration of SO_2 will increase and the concentration of O_2 will decrease.
    B. The concentration of O_2 will increase and the concentration of SO_2 will decrease.
    C. The concentration of SO_2 and O_2 will increase and the concentration of SO_3 will decrease.
    D. The concentration of SO_3 will increase and the concentration of SO_2 and O_2 will decrease.

13. Hospitals sometimes have outbreaks of staphylococcus bacteria infections that do not respond immediately to treatment with antibiotics that during earlier outbreaks were highly effective. Which of the following might explain this phenomenon?

    A. Selective forces have resulted in new staphylococcus strains that are resistant to antibiotics that were once effective.
    B. The antibiotics developed in recent years are weaker than antibiotics in use previously and are administered in smaller doses.
    C. Patients today are generally healthier and so have become less susceptible to staphylococcus bacteria infections over the years.
    D. Patients confined to a hospital environment in close proximity to other patients infected with staphylococcus are likely to contract the infection.

14. The wings of sparrows and flies are said to represent

    A. Homologous structures
    B. Analogous structures
    C. Vestigial structures
    D. Mimicry structures

Strategy Summary Sheet
Day Two PSAE—ISBE-Developed Science

STRUCTURE OF THE DAY TWO PSAE ISBE-DEVELOPED SCIENCE TEST: The ISBE-Developed Science Test is 40 minutes long with 45 multiple-choice questions. It is the first test given on the second day of the exam. The test is designed to assess the Illinois Learning Standard for science, which comprises inquiry; life sciences; physical sciences; Earth and space sciences; and science, technology, and society. The test uses questions from seven broad content areas:

(1) Biology
(2) Chemistry
(3) Physics
(4) Earth

(5) Space
(6) Ecology
(7) Society

- *Biology* questions ask students to know and apply concepts that explain how living things function, adapt, and change.

- *Chemistry* questions ask students to know and apply concepts that describe properties of matter and energy and the interactions between them.

- *Physics* questions ask students to know and apply concepts that describe force and motion and the principles that explain them.

- *Earth* questions ask students to know and apply concepts that describe the features and processes of the Earth and its resources.

- *Space* questions ask students to know and apply concepts that explain the composition and structure of the universe and the Earth's place in it.

- *Ecology* questions ask students to know and apply concepts that describe how living things interact with each other and with their environment.

- *Society* questions ask students to know and apply concepts that explain the effects of science and technology on social relationships.

Questions are distributed equally between the seven categories. While there is no general ladder of difficulty (increasing difficulty with increasing problem number), the questions tend to get harder toward the end of the test.

ISBE-DEVELOPED SCIENCE GENERAL STRATEGIES: The following are basic general ISBE-Developed Science strategies:

- *Read the question carefully.* It is important to read the questions carefully and to answer what is *actually* being asked by the test-writers.

- *Consider all the answer choices.* It is important that students examine all of the answer choices before choosing the

- *Carefully study any additional information.* Diagrams, tables, charts, *etc.*, may contain the information needed to answer the question.

- *Eliminate as many choices as possible.* Educated guessing, after eliminating as many answer choices as possible, is an important test-taking tool—even if students don't know the correct answer.

- *Use all of your knowledge.* This is a science test, assessing not only inquiry and analytical skills, but also acquired knowledge base and the ability to apply that knowledge to new situations. Therefore, use any information that you think is relevant.

ADDITIONAL NOTES AND STRATEGIES FROM IN-CLASS DISCUSSION: _____

_____

_____

_____

_____

_____

_____

_____

_____

_____

_____

_____

_____

_____

_____

_____

_____

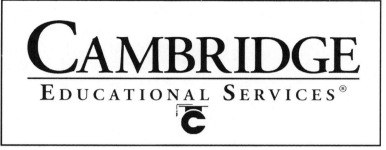

Day Two PSAE

APPLIED MATHEMATICS

AMERICA'S #1 STANDARDS-BASED SCHOOL IMPROVEMENT PROGRAM

Cambridge Course Concept Outline
STEP THREE

I. MATHEMATICS REFERENCE TABLE (p. 95)

II. SECTION ONE—APPLIED MATHEMATICS REVIEW (p. 96)

A. OVERVIEW OF THE APPLIED MATHEMATICS LESSON

B. INTRODUCTION TO THE APPLIED MATHEMATICS TEST

C. FORMAT OF THE APPLIED MATHEMATICS TEST

D. FIVE LEVELS OF QUESTION DIFFICULTY

    1. LEVEL 3 QUESTIONS
    2. LEVEL 4 QUESTIONS
    3. LEVEL 5 QUESTIONS
    4. LEVEL 6 QUESTIONS
    5. LEVEL 7 QUESTIONS

E. TEST-TAKING STRATEGIES

    1. WORK AS QUICKLY AS POSSIBLE
    2. READ THE QUESTION CAREFULLY
    3. PAY CAREFUL ATTENTION TO UNITS
    4. USE COMMON SENSE
    5. DON'T CHECK YOUR ARITHMETIC

F. PROBLEMS BY CATEGORY

    1. **SINGLE-STEP ARITHMETIC** (Review Questions #1-5, p. 96)
    2. **MULTI-STEP ARITHMETIC** (Review Questions #6-14, p. 96)
    3. **AVERAGE** (Review Questions #15-18, p. 98)
    4. **PERCENT** (Review Questions #19-21, p. 98)
    5. **AREA/PERIMETER** (Review Questions #22-23, p. 99)
    6. **VOLUME** (Review Question #24, p. 99)
    7. **BEST DEAL** (Review Questions #25-34, p. 99)
    8. **DIMENSIONAL ANALYSIS/MIXED UNITS**
       (Review Questions #35-48, p. 101)
    9. **CHALLENGE PROBLEMS** (Review Questions #49-60, p. 102)

MATHEMATICS REFERENCE TABLE

Units of Measurement

Distance
1 foot = 12 inches
1 yard = 3 feet
1 mile = 5,280 feet
1 mile ≈ 1.61 kilometers
1 inch ≈ 2.540 centimeters
1 foot ≈ 0.3048 meters
1 meter = 1,000 millimeters
1 meter = 100 centimeters
1 kilometer = 1,000 meters
1 kilometer ≈ 0.62 miles

Area
1 square foot = 144 square inches
1 square yard = 9 square feet
1 acre ≈ 208.71 feet square
1 acre = 43,560 square feet

Volume
1 cup = 8 fluid ounces
1 quart = 4 cups
1 gallon = 4 quarts
1 gallon = 231 cubic inches
1 liter ≈ 0.264 gallons
1 cubic foot = 1,728 cubic inches
1 cubic yard = 27 cubic feet
1 board foot = 1 inch by 12 inches by 12 inches

Weight
1 ounce ≈ 28.350 grams
1 pound = 16 ounces
1 pound = ≈ 453.593 grams
1 milligram = 0.001 grams
1 kilogram = 1,000 grams
1 kilogram ≈ 2.2 pounds
1 ton = 2,000 pounds

Temperature
$°C = 0.56(°F - 32)$ or $\frac{5}{9}(°F - 32)$
$°F = 1.8(°C) + 32$ or $(\frac{9}{5} \cdot °C) + 32$

Electricity
1 kilowatt-hour = 1,000 watt-hour

Formulas

Rectangle
perimeter = 2(*length* + *width*)
area = *length* • *width*

Cube
volume = (*length of side*)^3

Triangle
sum of angles = 180°
area of $\frac{1}{2}$(*base* • *height*)

Circle
number of degrees in a circle = 360°
circumference ≈ 3.14 • *diameter*
area ≈ 3.14 • (*radius*)^2

Cylinder
volume ≈ 3.14 • (*radius*)^2 • *height*

Cone
volume ≈ $\frac{3.14 \cdot (radius)^2 \cdot height}{3}$

Sphere
volume ≈ $\frac{4}{3}$ • 3.14 • (*radius*)^3

Amperage
Amps = *watts* ÷ *volts*

SECTION ONE—APPLIED MATHEMATICS REVIEW

DIRECTIONS: The questions in this section accompany the in-class review of the Applied Mathematics concepts and skills tested by the PSAE Applied Mathematics test. You will work through the questions with your instructor in class. Solve each problem and choose the best answer. You may use your calculator for any problems you choose, but some of the problems may best be done without using a calculator. Answers are on page 214.

1. Emily paid $1.69 (tax included) for a bag of potato chips. She gave the clerk a five-dollar bill. How much change should Emily receive?

   A. $8.31
   B. $3.69
   C. $3.31
   D. $2.21
   E. $1.69

2. You are filling bags with pieces of wood for a wooden toy factory. You have 576 pieces of wood and 6 bags. If you equally distribute the pieces of wood, how many pieces of wood will you put in each bag?

   A. 582
   B. 570
   C. 98
   D. 96
   E. 78

3. You hand a grocery clerk one dollar in order to purchase a candy bar that costs $.69. She gives you $.39 change. What is the error made by the clerk?

   A. The clerk gave you $.10 too much.
   B. The clerk gave you $.08 too much.
   C. The clerk gave you $.06 too little.
   D. The clerk gave you $.08 too little.
   E. The clerk gave you $.10 too little.

4. A grocery store charges $2.04 for a dozen bananas. If each banana costs the same amount, how much does one banana cost?

   A. 13 cents
   B. 14 cents
   C. 15 cents
   D. 16 cents
   E. 17 cents

5. A customer at the hardware store where you work bought 8 pounds of nails for 68 cents per pound. How much should you charge the customer?

   A. $4.88
   B. $5.44
   C. $6.12
   D. $6.98
   E. $8.12

6. Bob wants to buy a can of soda that costs 75 cents, but Bob only has 2 quarters. How many additional cents does Bob need to buy a can of soda?

   A. 25 cents
   B. 50 cents
   C. 55 cents
   D. 60 cents
   E. 75 cents

7. You have been sent out of the office to buy lunch for you and your four co-workers. Each of you wants the $1.99 (tax included) hamburger special. Exactly how much money will you need for the total bill?

   A. $1.99
   B. $3.98
   C. $5.97
   D. $7.96
   E. $9.95

8. Sarah works as a waitress in a restaurant. Her weekly earnings consist of her total hourly wage earnings, plus her tips. Her hourly wage is $6.01, and she worked 43 hours last week. She received the following amounts of tips last week: Monday, $12.25; Tuesday, $14.30; Wednesday, $11.50; Thursday, $12.10; Friday, $32.00. What was the total amount of Sarah's weekly earnings last week?

   A. $ 258.43
   B. $ 340.58
   C. $ 599.01
   D. $1,200.42
   E. $2,003.68

Item	Cost Per Item	Number of Items
Pencils	11 cents	8
Pads of Paper	59 cents	6

9. To get ready for school, Kendra purchased the items that are listed in the table above. How much did Kendra pay for all of the items?

A. $ .88
B. $3.54
C. $4.42
D. $5.38
E. $6.97

10. You have a budget of $2,100 for your day care center. You have to buy a play gym for the recreation room and put down new floor covering. The play gym costs $600. The room has dimensions of 12 feet by 30 feet. Play Safe Padding sells a carpet-like safety floor covering for $30 per square yard, plus an installation fee of $325. Child Proof sells square-foot safety tiles that you can install yourself. The cost is $4 per tile. If you choose the less expensive flooring option, how much money will be left over from your budget?

A. $ 60
B. $120
C. $150
D. $175
E. $225

11. As a security guard, you are assigned to stand watch at a turnstile at the only entrance and exit of an office. Your shift begins at 8:00 AM. When you arrive to work, the night guard tells you that there are 3 people in the office. By the time your shift is over at 5:00 PM, the meter on the turnstile shows that 38 people have entered the office and 31 people have left. How many people are in the office at 5:00 PM?

A. 3
B. 7
C. 10
D. 13
E. 21

12. Penny is scheduled to make four pizza deliveries. She leaves the store with 4 pizzas and $20.00. She collects $10.95 for the first pizza and is given a $2.00 tip. She collects $14.95 for the second pizza and is given a $2.00 tip. She collects $8.95 for the third pizza and is given a $1.50 tip. At her final delivery, she collects $14.95 for the fourth pizza and is given a $2.25 tip. How much money does Penny have when she returns to the store?

A. $52.80
B. $57.55
C. $77.55
D. $83.45
E. $84.45

13. You went to the hardware store to buy electrical outlets and boxes for a job. You paid for 25 outlets and 15 boxes at a cost of $4.95 per outlet and $1.29 per box, plus 6% sales tax. When you got back to the job, you found that your order contained only 20 outlets and 12 boxes. How much money had you been overcharged?

A. $ 3.87
B. $24.75
C. $28.32
D. $30.34
E. $36.73

14. Mary Kate is supposed to earn $6.75 per hour. Last week, she worked 32 hours and was paid $212.50. How much did that figure differ from what Mary Kate's total pay should have been?

A. The employer's calculation was $6.75 too little.
B. The employer's calculation was $4.50 too little.
C. The employer's calculation was $3.50 too little.
D. The employer's calculation was $2.50 too little.
E. The employer's calculation was $3.50 too much.

15. You do consulting work for a test preparation firm. The owner has asked you to submit the total number of hours that you worked last week. You worked the following hours: Monday, 1.2 hours; Tuesday, 1.4 hours; Wednesday, 7.6 hours; Thursday, 8 hours; and Friday, 0.5 hours. How many total hours did you work for the test preparation firm last week?

    A. 18.7
    B. 18.9
    C. 19.1
    D. 19.3
    E. 19.5

16. Deirdre has taken seven exams this semester. Her scores are as follows: 81, 81, 83, 81, 91, 94, and 98. What is Deirdre's average exam score?

    A. 81
    B. 83
    C. 85
    D. 87
    E. 89

17. You are a dental assistant. Last week, you treated 8 patients on Monday, 12 on Tuesday, 9 on Wednesday, 6 on Thursday, and 12 on Friday. What was the average number of patients that you treated on a daily basis?

    A. 8.6
    B. 9.4
    C. 10.2
    D. 11
    E. 12.3

18. You are a delivery driver with a daily route. On Monday, it took 6 hours and 45 minutes to run the route; on Tuesday, it took 7 hours and 18 minutes; on Wednesday, it took 5 hours and 55 minutes; on Thursday, it took 8 hours and 12 minutes; and on Friday, it took 7 hours and 15 minutes. What was the average time that it took you to run the route that week?

    A. 5 hours and 25 minutes
    B. 5 hours and 45 minutes
    C. 6 hours and 18 minutes
    D. 6 hours and 27 minutes
    E. 7 hours and 5 minutes

19. Amy is the owner of a company that makes basketball equipment. She is interviewing two potential employees for the sales department. Amy estimates that the first candidate could sell $52,000 worth of equipment per month and she would need to pay him a 9% sales commission. She estimates that the second candidate could sell $50,400 worth of equipment per month and she would need to pay her an 8% sales commission. What is the most money that Amy could make for her company per month on the equipment sold by one of these two potential salespersons?

    A. $50,400
    B. $47,320
    C. $46,840
    D. $46,368
    E. $46,268

20. You are the payroll accountant for your firm. Felix Ortiz, who has been with the firm for six months, has been given a 15% raise that becomes effective during the next pay-period. If Felix currently earns $10.40 per hour, what will be his new hourly pay after the raise is applied?

    A. $ 1.56
    B. $ 9.26
    C. $11.96
    D. $12.72
    E. $25.40

21. Jim is a real estate agent who is selling a house for a client. After paying off the $108,000 balance on the mortgage, his client needs to have at least $30,000 remaining for a down payment on a new house. If Jim's commission is 8% of the selling price, what is the lowest possible price that his client should accept?

    A. $150,000
    B. $145,000
    C. $142,500
    D. $140,000
    E. $138,000

22. You are painting a rectangular floor that is 18 feet long by 12 feet wide. One can of paint is required to cover 8 square yards. If each can of paint costs $14.95 (tax included), how much money do you need to spend on paint in order to cover the floor?

   A. $ 29.00
   B. $ 44.85
   C. $ 59.80
   D. $ 74.75
   E. $414.95

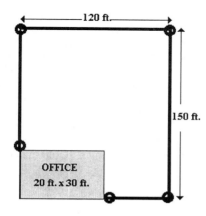

23. You are planning to open a new landscaping business. As part of the preparation, you are putting a fence around a rectangular yard where equipment will be kept, as shown by the dark, heavy line in the diagram above. If fencing costs $10 per linear foot, what is the cost of the fence?

   A. $ 490
   B. $2,200
   C. $2,700
   D. $4,900
   E. $5,400

24. Andy packs 3 balls into a cylindrical can. Each ball has a radius of 3.2 centimeters. The inside radius of the can is 3.4 centimeters, and the inside height of the can is 19.5 centimeters. Approximately how many cubic inches of the interior of the can are NOT composed of tennis balls?

   A. 4.38 cubic inches
   B. 6.68 cubic inches
   C. 11.04 cubic inches
   D. 15.96 cubic inches
   E. 18.18 cubic inches

25. The table below shows the mileage that you drove on your delivery route for each day in a week. Your van gets 12 miles per gallon of gasoline. If gasoline cost you $1.62 per gallon, what was the cost of the gasoline that you used for the week?

Monday	12 miles
Tuesday	17 miles
Wednesday	13 miles
Thursday	8 miles
Friday	10 miles

   A. $5.00
   B. $8.10
   C. $12.60
   D. $15.30
   E. $60.00

26. One of your duties in your job at the bookstore is ordering books from wholesalers. Two wholesalers offer *The Complete Dictionary*, which has a cover price of $28.00, at the following discounts off the cover price:

DISCOUNTS OFF $28 LIST PRICE			
MegaBooks, Inc.		*Academic Press, Inc.*	
1 to 5 copies	25% discount on each copy	1 to 10 copies	20% discount on each copy
6 to 10 copies	30% discount on each copy	11 to 20 copies	25% discount on each copy
11 or more copies	40% discount on each copy	20 or more copies	30% discount on each copy
Add $2 per copy for shipping		Shipping included	

You plan to order 30 copies. Which of the following statements is true about the order?

   A. MegaBooks will be $60 less than Academic Press
   B. MegaBooks will be $24 less than Academic Press
   C. MegaBooks will be $26 more than Academic Press
   D. MegaBooks will be $30 more than Academic Press
   E. MegaBooks will be $84 more than Academic Press

27. You are installing a hardwood floor in a rectangular room with dimensions of 10 feet by 18 feet. The product instructions say to allow an additional 10% of material for waste. If the flooring comes in boxes containing 25 square feet each, how many boxes should you order to do the job?

    A. 5
    B. 6
    C. 7
    D. 8
    E. 9

28. The Rapid Delivery package service charges $12 for a pickup and $8 per package. The Express package service charges $20 for a pickup and $5 per package. If you have a pickup consisting of 8 packages, how much will you save if you use Express rather than Rapid Delivery?

    A. $ 4
    B. $12
    C. $16
    D. $24
    E. $75

29. A taxi cab in Morristown charges $2.50 for the first mile and $0.20 for each additional $\frac{1}{4}$ mile. A taxi cab in Clementville charges $2.00 for the first $\frac{1}{5}$ mile and $0.25 for each additional $\frac{1}{5}$ mile. What is the difference in cost between a 5-mile taxi ride in Morristown and a 5-mile ride in Clementville?

    A. $1.30
    B. $1.70
    C. $2.35
    D. $4.10
    E. $4.85

30. You are in charge of purchasing toilet tissue for your place of employment. You need to purchase 120 rolls of toilet tissue. You can buy a four-pack for $1.29, a twelve-pack for $3.69, or a twenty-four-pack for $7.19. How much will you save on the 120 rolls if you choose the most economical option rather than the most expensive option?

    A. $1.20
    B. $1.80
    C. $2.20
    D. $2.75
    E. $3.05

31. You are ordering new keyboards for the computers in your office. The K10 model costs $15.95, and the K15 model costs $19.45. Originally, you planned to order 12 K10 keyboards and 8 K15 keyboards but changed the order to specify 15 K10 keyboards and 5 K15 keyboards. How much money did you save by changing the order?

    A. $ 3.45
    B. $ 8.75
    C. $ 10.50
    D. $336.50
    E. $347.00

32. You are considering one of three cell phone plans. The first plan costs $19.95 per month, plus 5.4 cents for each minute used per month. The second plan costs $29.95 per month, plus 6.1 cents for each minute used per month after the first 200 minutes. The third plan costs $34.95 per month for unlimited calling. The average number of minutes used per month is 243. Based on this average, how much would the cheapest plan cost per month?

    A. $29.95
    B. $32.57
    C. $33.07
    D. $34.86
    E. $34.95

33. Kathryn has been offered 3 jobs. The first job pays $6.25 per hour for the first 6 weeks and $6.50 per hour for the next 6 weeks. The second job pays $6.30 per hour for the first 8 weeks and $6.55 per hour for the next 4 weeks. The third job pays $6.35 per hour for the first 10 weeks and $6.75 per hour for the next 2 weeks. If Kathryn works 40 hours each week, how much more will she earn over the 12-week period if she accepts the most profitable job offer rather than the least profitable job offer?

    A. $ 4
    B. $ 8
    C. $12
    D. $16
    E. $20

34. Your mother has sent you out to fill her prescription for 30 pills. Drugstore A will sell 10 pills for $14.97, plus 5% tax. Drugstore B will sell 15 pills for $20.79, plus 5% tax. Drugstore C will sell 30 pills for $43.78, plus 5% tax. What is the least amount of money that you would pay to have your mother's prescription filled at one of the three drugstores?

   A. $43.66
   B. $45.97
   C. $47.16
   D. $49.04
   E. $49.07

35. Each morning, you take the train to your job in the city. If the train leaves the station at 7:13 AM and the trip takes 54 minutes, at what time does the train arrive in the city?

   A. 7:57 AM
   B. 8:03 AM
   C. 8:07 AM
   D. 8:17 AM
   E. 8:22 AM

36. Yesterday, Jenny left school at 11:45 AM for lunch and returned to school at 12:30 PM. How long did Jenny take for her lunch break?

   A. 45 minutes
   B. 55 minutes
   C. 65 minutes
   D. 75 minutes
   E. 85 minutes

37. In your job at the bookstore, you fill orders and calculate the shipping weight. The hardcover edition of *The Complete Dictionary* weighs 3 pounds and 12 ounces. The paperback edition weighs 1 pound and 4 ounces. If an order consists of three copies of the hardcover edition and two copies of the paperback edition, what is the shipping weight of the order?

   A. 5 pounds
   B. 5 pounds 8 ounces
   C. 6 pounds 4 ounces
   D. 12 pounds 8 ounces
   E. 13 pounds 12 ounces

38. You have purchased five melons from the grocery store. The first melon weighs 3 pounds, 3 ounces; the second weighs 3 pounds, 5 ounces; the third weighs 2 pounds, 15 ounces; the fourth weighs 2 pounds, 14 ounces; and the fifth weighs 3 pounds, 10 ounces. What is the average weight of the five melons?

   A. 2 pounds, 15 ounces
   B. 3 pounds, 1 ounce
   C. 3 pounds, 3 ounces
   D. 3 pounds, 7 ounces
   E. 4 pounds, 2 ounces

39. You are working in a factory and have been given the job of breaking down old boxes. You estimate that it will take you about 52 seconds to break down each box. If there are 30 old boxes, about how many seconds will it take you to break them all down?

   A. 1.73 seconds
   B. 22 seconds
   C. 82 seconds
   D. 1,508 seconds
   E. 1,560 seconds

40. Each can of your company's product weighs 1 pound, 2 ounces. Your employer instructs you not to exceed 8 kilograms per box when you pack the cans. What is the maximum number of cans that you can put into a box?

   A. 12
   B. 13
   C. 14
   D. 15
   E. 16

41. You purchased a 1,122-yard by 854-yard rectangular field for $44,148.00. Approximately how much did you pay per acre for the field?

   A. $147.00
   B. $148.00
   C. $223.00
   D. $248.00
   E. $343.00

42. At the bakery, apple pies are baked in a 400°F oven for 40 minutes. At 10:10 AM, a tray of pies baking in the oven is half-baked. At what time will the pies finish baking?

    A. 10:15 AM
    B. 10:20 AM
    C. 10:25 AM
    D. 10:30 AM
    E. 10:50 AM

43. Jim is in the lawn mowing business. It takes him 1.3 hours to mow a lawn. How long would it take Jim to mow 6 lawns?

    A. 7.8 hours
    B. 7.3 hours
    C. 4.7 hours
    D. 4.62 hours
    E. 4.3 hours

44. Yesterday, you drank the following liquids: an eight-ounce glass of milk, a six-ounce glass of orange juice, one quart of water, one pint of Pepsi, and one pint of Coke. How many ounces of liquid did you drink?

    A. 112 ounces
    B. 110 ounces
    C. 88 ounces
    D. 78 ounces
    E. 76 ounces

45. You have been asked to paint the entire outside of a rectangular container with dimensions of 4 feet by 6 feet by 8 feet. One quart of paint will cover 5 square yards. What is the minimum number of quart-sized cans of paint that you will need?

    A. 3
    B. 4
    C. 5
    D. 6
    E. 7

46. Using your garden hose, you can water your 43-foot by 28-foot rectangular lawn in 7 minutes and 20 seconds. About how long would it take you to water your neighbor's 68-foot by 37-foot rectangular lawn if you work at the same speed per square foot as you do on your own lawn?

    A. 12 minutes and 13 seconds
    B. 15 minutes and 19 seconds
    C. 16 minutes and 12 seconds
    D. 16 minutes and 23 seconds
    E. 17 minutes and 14 seconds

47. You are an assistant chef at a restaurant. It takes you 20 minutes to prepare 80 orders of eggplant parmigiana. How many minutes would it take you to prepare 120 orders of eggplant parmigiana?

    A. 10
    B. 12
    C. 15
    D. 28
    E. 30

48. When Jessica serves spaghetti, she uses one jar of sauce for every six plates. At Jessica's most recent dinner party, she served a plate of spaghetti to each of the 54 guests. How many jars of sauce did Jessica need?

    A. 9
    B. 10
    C. 11
    D. 12
    E. 13

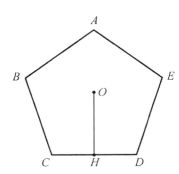

49. John is employed by a painting company, and he is painting the floor pictured above; it is in the shape of a regular pentagon (all five sides have the same length and all five angles have the same number of degrees). John knows that point O is at the center of the pentagon and that point H lies halfway between points C and D. He has already used 1.22 quarts of paint to cover triangle OHD. If paint can only be purchased in quart-sized cans, what is the minimum number of additional quart-sized cans of paint that John will need to cover the entire pentagon?

    A. 1
    B. 2
    C. 10
    D. 11
    E. 51

50. Last week, you worked 46 hours and sold $7,324 worth of goods for your company. You have been offered three choices for the pay that you will receive:

I. A flat rate of $13.46 per hour with no commission
II. A rate of $12.43 per hour, plus a 5% commission on all merchandise over $4,300 that you sold during the week
III. A rate of $11.12 per hour, plus a 2.6% commission on all merchandise that you sold during the week

How much more will you be paid if you choose the alternative in which you make the most amount of money rather than the alternative in which you make the least amount of money?

A. $ 46.48
B. $103.82
C. $619.16
D. $622.98
E. $701.94

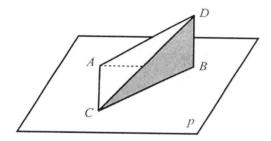

51. Allyson is an architect, and she has made the scale drawing above. In her scale drawing, DB = 1.68 inches, AB = 4.35 inches, and AC = 2.50 inches. The line from point D to point B makes a right angle with the plane labeled as p, and the line from point A to point B makes a right angle with the line from point A to point C on the plane. The solid figure labeled $ACBD$ is a right pyramid. If the scale is 1 inch = 23 feet for the actual pyramid, then the total volume of the pyramid contains approximately how many cubic feet? Note: the volume of a pyramid is $\frac{1}{3}$ times the area of the base times the height of the pyramid.

A. 22,048
B. 28,113
C. 32,448
D. 35,676
E. 37,049

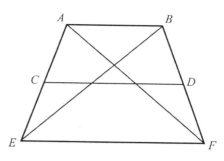

52. You have applied for a job that requires some imaginative thinking. Your employer shows you the figure above, tells you that the top and bottom line segments are parallel, and gives you the following lengths: AB = 314.6, AC = 307.8, CE = 308.7, BD = 307.8, DF = 308.7, and EF = 468.4. You are then asked to determine the exact length from point C to point D. Since the top and bottom are parallel, and $AE = BF$, the distance from point C to point D will be the average of the top and bottom lengths. Therefore, what is the exact distance from point C to point D?

A. 307.8
B. 308.7
C. 314.6
D. 391.5
E. 403.2

53. You have a total budget of $1,500 for the next 20 years to buy a new coffeemaker and new carpeting for the floor in the office lounge. The floor is 15 feet by 24 feet. The DELUXE coffeemaker costs $89.95, and you estimate that it will last for 10 years. The ULTIMATE coffeemaker costs $174.95, and you estimate that it will last for 20 years. ABC Warehouse sells carpet that will last for 5 years at $5 per square yard, plus $110 for installation. DEF Warehouse sells carpet that will last for 10 years at $12.05 per square yard, plus $125 for installation. GHJ Warehouse sells carpet that will last for 20 years at $28.95 per square yard, plus $165 for installation. Assuming that your estimates are correct and that prices will not change over the 20-year period, about how much of the total budget would remain if you make the most economical choice for the entire 20-year period?

A. $111.05
B. $ 98.45
C. $ 67.35
D. $ 15.15
E. $ 2.05

54. Company A offers you a starting yearly salary of $64,000. They promise that you will be given a raise of 5% over the previous year's salary for the next 4 years thereafter. Company B offers you a starting yearly salary of $65,000. They promise that you will be given a raise of $3,250 over the previous year's salary for the next 4 years thereafter. How much more total salary for 5 years will you earn if you accept the better offer?

    A. $13,000
    B. $12,000
    C. $ 5,000
    D. $ 4,875.50
    E. $ 3,859.60

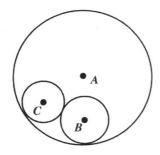

55. If the lengths of the radii of circles A, B, and C are 23 feet, 8 feet, and 7 feet, respectively, then what is the total distance from A to B to C and back to A?

    A. 38 feet
    B. 40 feet
    C. 42 feet
    D. 44 feet
    E. 46 feet

56. You are talking with three different banks about purchasing a home for $400,000. The first bank says that they will give you a 30-year mortgage with a payment of $2,935.06 per month. The second bank says that they will give you a 25-year mortgage with a payment of $2,827.12 per month. The third bank says that they will give you a 20-year mortgage with a payment of $2,982.25 per month. What is the difference between the greatest total payout and the least total payout of the three choices?

    A. $340,881.60
    B. $208,485.60
    C. $113,232.50
    D. $112,232.50
    E. $ 56,616.25

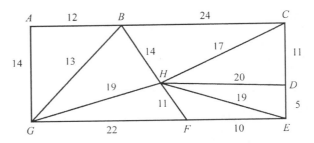

57. Your employer instructs you to drive a certain number of miles from point A to point E via the shortest route shown on the map above. How many miles is the shortest route from point A to point E?

    A. 44 miles
    B. 45 miles
    C. 46 miles
    D. 47 miles
    E. 48 miles

58. The best shooter at your high school makes an average of 61 three-pointers out of every 100 attempts. Last week, you attempted 100 three-pointers on Monday, Tuesday, Wednesday, and Thursday, and you made the following number of shots, respectively: 59, 57, 58, and 63. If you attempted 100 three-pointers on Friday, how many must you have made in order that your average for the five days was equal to the best shooter at your high school?

    A. 65
    B. 66
    C. 67
    D. 68
    E. 69

59. Your company operates a ferry service between City A and City B. The service uses two ferries. One ferry leaves City A and sails on a direct course to City B at 20 miles per hour. The other ferry leaves City B at the same time and sails on a direct course to City A at 25 miles per hour. How far apart are City A and City B if the two ferries pass each other after exactly 30 minutes?

    A.   8 miles
    B.   12 miles
    C.   17.5 miles
    D.   19 miles
    E.   22.5 miles

60. In your shop, you have a copy machine that can produce 30 copies per minute, a second machine that can produce 25 copies per minute, and a third machine than can produce 45 copies per minute. All three machines operating at the same time can do a job in 5 minutes. How many pages do they produce?

    A. 275
    B. 325
    C. 390
    D. 460
    E. 500

SECTION TWO—APPLIED MATHEMATICS PROBLEM-SOLVING

DIRECTIONS: This section contains Applied Mathematics problems for in-class problem-solving with your instructor. Solve each problem and choose the best answer. You may use your calculator for any problems you choose, but some of the problems may best be done without using a calculator. Answers are on page 214.

1. In your job at the hardware store, a customer gives you a $20 bill to pay for a hammer that costs $7.98 and a box of nails that costs $1.69. How much change should you give back?

   A. $9.67
   B. $10.33
   C. $12.02
   D. $16.23
   E. $18.31

2. It takes you 1 hour to unload 15 pallets from a truck and stack them in the warehouse. On the average, how many minutes does it take to unload and stack 1 pallet?

   A. 4
   B. 6
   C. 12
   D. 20
   E. 60

3. Your copy machine at the printing shop takes 1 hour to copy 3,000 pages. On the average, how many seconds does it take the machine to copy 1 page?

   A. 1.2
   B. 1.5
   C. 2
   D. 2.5
   E. 3

4. In your position in the shipping room, you must assemble lots of boxes for packing. Some of the boxes weigh 2 pounds, some weigh 2 pounds 4 ounces, and some weigh 2 pounds 12 ounces. The maximum shipping weight of the contents of any one crate cannot exceed 21 pounds with any combination of packages. What is the greatest number of boxes that you can put into any one crate?

   A. 3
   B. 6
   C. 8
   D. 9
   E. 10

Item	Regular Price	Sale Price
Hamburger	$1.49	$1.19
French-fries	$1.19	$0.79
Milkshake	$2.19	$1.59

5. Each Friday night after the basketball game, you go to the concession stand to purchase a hamburger, an order of French fries, and a milkshake for each member of your team. On this particular occasion, there is a sale on all of these items. You purchase 18 hamburgers, 16 orders of French fries, and 18 milkshakes for your team. As a result of the sale, what is the overall percentage in savings?

   A. 26.5%
   B. 26.7%
   C. 26.9%
   D. 27.1%
   E. 27.3%

Time	Change from Previous Reading
9:00 AM	+3 pounds per square inch
10:00 AM	-7 pounds per square inch
11:00 AM	+2 pounds per square inch
12:00 PM	-1 pound per square inch

6. One of your responsibilities as a lab assistant is to read an air pressure gauge every hour and enter the changes in a logbook. The figure above shows the entries for four readings. What was the net change of the reading on the gauge over the time shown?

   A. decrease of 3 pounds per square inch
   B. decrease of 2 pounds per square inch
   C. increase of 2 pounds per square inch
   D. increase of 3 pounds per square inch
   E. increase of 5 pounds per square inch

7. Your job at the meat packing plant requires you to monitor the temperature of the giant cooler, but the thermometer on the thermostat is uncalibrated and reads 8° higher than the actual temperature in the cooler. When you check the thermostat, you find that the thermometer reads 42°F. The temperature inside the cooler should be 28°F. What should you do?

   A. Raise the temperature setting on the thermometer by 8°
   B. Raise the temperature setting on the thermometer by 6°
   C. Lower the temperature setting on the thermometer by 6°
   D. Lower the temperature setting on the thermometer to 8°
   E. Lower the temperature setting on the thermometer to 12°

8. You are preparing to paint a large storeroom that has four walls. Two of the walls measure $8\frac{1}{2}$ feet by 12 feet; the other two walls measure $8\frac{1}{2}$ feet by 15 feet. You will also paint the ceiling but not the floor. There are no windows, and you will paint the inside of the door as well. A quart of the paint you are using covers 150 square feet. How many quarts of paint should you buy to make sure that you have enough to complete the job?

   A. 1
   B. 3
   C. 5
   D. 7
   E. 9

9. You are working on a landscaping project that involves filling a raised, circular flower bed with topsoil to a depth of 9 inches. The radius of the bed is 8 feet. Approximately how many cubic feet of topsoil do you need for the job?

   A. 48
   B. 64
   C. 125
   D. 136
   E. 151

10. Your company has a conical tank that has a base radius of 9.6 feet and a height of 23.4 feet. Approximately how many gallons of water will this conical tank hold?

   A. 117 gallons
   B. 1,407 gallons
   C. 1,524 gallons
   D. 16,885 gallons
   E. 19,217 gallons

NOTES AND STRATEGIES

SECTION THREE—APPLIED MATHEMATICS QUIZZES

DIRECTIONS: This section contains three Applied Mathematics quizzes. Complete each quiz while being timed. Answers are on page 214.

QUIZ I (10 questions; 15 minutes)

1. You are working as a cashier. A customer makes a purchase for $5.12 and gives you a $10 bill. How much change should you give back?

   A. $1.76
   B. $3.49
   C. $4.88
   D. $5.62
   E. $6.14

2. The foreman at the plywood mill tells you to place sheets of plywood $\frac{3}{4}$ inches thick on top of one another to make stacks no higher than 4 feet. What is the maximum number of sheets of plywood that you can put in one stack?

   A. 3
   B. 5
   C. 12
   D. 48
   E. 64

3. Jane charges $10.00 per document, plus 32 cents per page. Hal charges $8.00 per document, plus 40 cents per page. Betty charges 53 cents per page for the first 20 pages and 23 cents for each additional page. You need a 51-page document typed. How much will it cost if you choose the least expensive of the three choices?

   A. $ 6.47
   B. $ 17.73
   C. $ 26.32
   D. $ 28.40
   E. $568.41

4. In your position as transportation supervisor for a school, you report on the number of students who ride the buses to school. During one week, your records show:

Bus #101—Ridership for Week 12	
Monday	23
Tuesday	27
Wednesday	33
Thursday	35
Friday	27

   For this bus, what was the average number of riders per day for the week?

   A. 24
   B. 26
   C. 27
   D. 29
   E. 34

5. Your business processes electronic transactions for a web business, and you receive a commission equal to 3% of the total value of the orders processed. If your business processes a transaction with a value of $1,200.00, what will your commission be?

   A. $30
   B. $36
   C. $150
   D. $360
   E. $420

6. Your new pair of glasses costs $81.23. You paid for the glasses with 5 twenty-dollar bills. How much money should you be given in change?

   A. $11.23
   B. $11.77
   C. $18.77
   D. $21.23
   E. $21.77

7. George has entered an eating contest. He must either eat 12 hamburgers or 25 hot dogs. George knows that he can eat a total of 2 hamburgers every 5.34 minutes and that he can eat a total of 5 hot dogs every 5.86 minutes. How many total minutes will George save if he chooses the alternative that takes the least amount of time rather than the alternative that takes the most amount of time?

   A. 0.52 minutes
   B. 2.74 minutes
   C. 3.34 minutes
   D. 5.68 minutes
   E. 29.3 minutes

8. You have $4,500 to carpet and furnish your company's conference room with a table and chairs. The carpet that you have already ordered costs $1,600 installed. Furniture Supreme offers a conference table for $1,110 plus 8 chairs for $245 per chair. Office Comforts offers a conference table plus 8 chairs for a total price of $2840. If you choose the less expensive table and chairs, how much, if anything, will be left in your budget?

   A. $60
   B. $230
   C. $822
   D. $912
   E. You will be $170 over budget

9. The paving company that you work for is selling a grader at auction. You hope to realize at least $24,000 from the sale of the grader after paying off an $18,000 loan still owed to the bank and after the commission charged by the auction house which is equal to 8% of the winning bid. If you plan to set an auction reserve (price below which the machine will not be sold), what should be the approximate reserve price?

   A. $34,780
   B. $35,110
   C. $39,410
   D. $42,110
   E. $45,652

10. Your firm uses an Internet data base called Infocom which charges $1.29 for each minute of connect time and $3.15 for each gigabyte of data transmitted. Another firm, Databit, charges $0.98 for each minute of connect time and $2.45 for each gigabyte of data transmitted. Last month your firm was billed by Infocom for 93 minutes of connect time and 43 gigabytes of data. If this usage is typical, what approximate percentage of your bill could you save by switching to Databit?

   A. 23%
   B. 34%
   C. 42%
   D. 58%
   E. 72%

QUIZ II (10 questions; 15 minutes)

1. In a typical week, you work 40 hours with no overtime. Your salary before taxes and other deductions is $334.00. How much do you make per hour?

   A. $6.25
   B. $7.48
   C. $8.35
   D. $9.12
   E. $10.17

2. Customers at the deli counter of grocery stores are not supposed to be charged for the weight of the plastic food container that is 2 ounces. If the weight of an order including the food and the container is 1 pound 1 ounce, what is the weight for which the customer should be charged?

   A. 15 ounces
   B. 1 pound 1 ounce
   C. 1 pound 2 ounces
   D. 2 pounds 1 ounce
   E. 2 pounds 4 ounces

3. In your job at the employment office, you give each applicant a multiple-choice test with 20 questions. Applicants get +1 point for each right answer and $-\frac{1}{4}$ point for each wrong answer.

   Blanks are not counted. What score should you give an applicant who answers 12 questions correctly, misses 4, and leaves 4 blank?

   A. 4
   B. 8
   C. 10
   D. 11
   E. 16

4. At your job, you operate a printing press. For one order, you must print 15,000 copies of a book. If it takes the machine 2 hours and 24 minutes to print 5,000 copies, how long will it take to print the entire order?

   A. 1 hour
   B. 4 hours, 48 minutes
   C. 6 hours, 24 minutes
   D. 7 hours, 12 minutes
   E. 8 hours, 36 minutes

5. At your fast-food restaurant, a customer can get a Tuesday-Nite special that offers a second meal at 50% off for each meal ordered. If a customer buys two orders of a meal that ordinarily cost $4.98 per meal and has a coupon for an additional $1.00 off the price after all other discounts, how much money should the customer be charged for the two meals?

   A. $6.47
   B. $7.11
   C. $7.49
   D. $8.47
   E. $9.12

6. In your job, you are in charge of ordering office supplies. You have been told to expect that a large project will require substantial use of the copy machine, and you need to buy 16 toner cartridges. The local office supply store sells one cartridge for $24.80 plus 5% sales tax. An Internet company charges no tax and sells one cartridge for $24.15. The Internet company charges a total of $20.00 in shipping for an entire order. If you choose the cheaper of the two sources, how much will you pay for 16 cartridges?

   A. $156.24
   B. $386.40
   C. $406.40
   D. $416.64
   E. $512.36

7. Every week, you must report to accounting the time that you have spent working on each account. On Monday, you spent 2 hours 37 minutes on the Hawkins account, on Tuesday, 3 hours 44 minutes, on Wednesday, 1 hour 15 minutes, on Thursday, 4 hours 56 minutes, and on Friday, 2 hours 23 minutes. For the week, what was the average time you spent on the Hawkins account?

   A. 89.5 minutes
   B. 1 hour, 18 minutes
   C. 2 hours, 59 minutes
   D. 3 hours, 17 minutes
   E. 177 hours

Check Number	Date	Memo	Check Amount	Deposit Amount	Balance
	3/1	Deposit	—	$1,000.00	$1,000.00
101	3/3	Insurance	$75.00	—	$
102	3/10	Supplies	$423.17	—	$
103	3/26	Postage	$27.32	—	$
104	3/27	Rent	$335.50	—	$
	3/31	Deposit	—	$230.55	$

8. On March 1st, you opened a new checking account for your cleaning service business. Based on the check register above, how much money is in the account on April 1st?

   A. $91.54
   B. $139.01
   C. $369.56
   D. $413.27
   E. $860.90

9. The crafts shop where you work sells decorative candles made by filling a cylindrical mold with a liquid plastic compound that eventually hardens. The mold is 4 inches in diameter and 12 inches high, and the liquid plastic compound comes in 1-gallon containers. If you plan to make 2 dozen candles, how many 1-gallon containers of the liquid plastic compound will you need for the job?

   A. 4
   B. 8
   C. 16
   D. 24
   E. 30

10. Your printing firm ordinarily pays $1.32 per gallon for standard black ink. In a trade publication, you found an advertisement by a supply company that offers the same product for 34 cents per liter. If you are thinking of spending a total of $118.80 on ink with your usual supplier, approximately how much would it cost to buy a similar amount of ink from the other company?

   A. $90.00
   B. $115.90
   C. $225.40
   D. $315.68
   E. $340.90

QUIZ III (11 questions; 15 minutes)

1. In your job as a driver for a delivery company, you deliver and pickup packages along your route. At 8:00 am, you leave the central office with 48 packages. By the time you return at 5:00 pm, you have delivered 46 packages and picked up 18 packages. How many packages do you have on your truck at 5:00 pm?

   A. 16
   B. 20
   C. 26
   D. 27
   E. 30

2. You are relieved from your position as a machine operator at the plant at 11:25 a.m. for a 50-minute lunch break. When must you begin working again?

   A. 11:30
   B. 11:45
   C. 11:50
   D. 12:05
   E. 12:15

3. As manager of the Pizza Parlor, it is your responsibility to make the dough from a recipe that calls for 3 quarts of water for every 5 pounds of flour. If the recipe makes enough dough to make 20 pizzas, and you need to make 50 pizzas, how many pounds of flour should you use?

   A. $2\frac{1}{2}$
   B. $7\frac{1}{2}$
   C. $10\frac{1}{2}$
   D. $12\frac{1}{2}$
   E. 15

4. At the garden center where you work, it takes you 20 seconds to plant 3 seedbeds. How long will it take you to plant 30 such seedbeds?

   A. 1 minute, 30 seconds
   B. 2 minutes, 40 seconds
   C. 3 minutes, 20 seconds
   D. 4 minutes, 10 seconds
   E. 5 minutes, 30 seconds

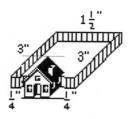

5. You are building a stockade fence around the backyard of a city row house according to the diagram shown above. On the drawing, each inch represents 10 feet of fence. What will be the total length of the fence, in feet?

   A. 20 feet
   B. 30 feet
   C. 50 feet
   D. 80 feet
   E. 100 feet

6. As part of your job at the mill, you are filling a vat with a chemical solution. Two pipes, each operating independently, fill the vat, one at the rate of 30 gallons per minute and the other at the rate of 40 gallons per minute. If it takes exactly 8 minutes to fill the vat with solution, how many gallons does the vat hold?

   A. 240
   B. 340
   C. 560
   D. 580
   E. 620

7. You are going to treat a lawn using a liquid fertilizer spreader. The fertilizer must be diluted with an amount of water equal to 2/5 of its original volume. Ten gallons of the liquid fertilizer treat an area of 300 square feet and, after dilution, one-fourth more area. The lawn to be treated is 1,440 square feet. If you dilute the fertilizer as required, how many 10-gallon drums of the liquid fertilizer must you buy?

   A. 1 drum
   B. 2 drums
   C. 3 drums
   D. 4 drums
   E. 5 drums

Overnight Rates			
Fast Delivery Service		Urgent Express Company	
up to 8 ounces	$12.00	up to 1 pound	$7.50
over 8 ounces to 1 pound	$0.75 for every additional ounce or part of an ounce	over 1 pound to 2 pounds	$1.00 for every additional ounce or part of an ounce
over 1 pound	$0.50 for every additional ounce or part of an ounce	over 2 pounds	$0.75 for every additional ounce or part of an ounce

8. Your job requires you to choose the cheapest way of sending important documents via overnight courier. The above table shows the rates of the two couriers used by your firm. Using the cheaper method of shipping, what will be the cost of shipping a package weighing 3 pounds?

A. $16.25
B. $18.75
C. $23.00
D. $34.00
E. $35.50

9. Your car has a 16-gallon gas tank. There is a gas station within a few hundred feet of your house, so you fill the gas tank whenever you return home with fewer than 4 gallons remaining. Assume that you get 25 miles per gallon. On Monday, you started with a full tank and drove 325 miles. On Tuesday, you drove 100 miles. On Wednesday, you drove 50 miles. On Thursday, you drove 75 miles. On Friday, you drove 125 miles. On Saturday, you drove 350 miles. On how many of these six days did you fill the gas tank upon returning home?

A. 2
B. 3
C. 4
D. 5
E. 6

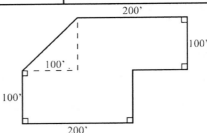

10. The cooperative extension where you work is testing some new seed hybrids. The field shown in the diagram above must be seeded with grass. The plan calls for coverage of 1.45 pounds of grass seed per 100 square feet. The seed comes in 80 pound bags in which 40% of the material by weight is inert material and the rest is grass seed. How many bags of seed will you need?

A. 14
B. 23
C. 137
D. 425
E. 1,510

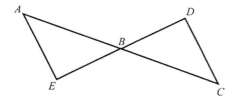

11. You are to paint the design that consists of two triangles of the same size as pictured above. You know that the triangles have right angles at point E and at point D. The distance from point A to point E is 5 feet, and the distance from point B to point E is 6 feet. One can of paint will cover 8.42 square feet. What is the minimum number of cans of paint that you will need to paint the design?

A. 1
B. 4
C. 6
D. 7
E. 9

AMERICA'S #1 STANDARDS-BASED SCHOOL IMPROVEMENT PROGRAM

Strategy Summary Sheet
Day Two PSAE—Applied Mathematics

STRUCTURE OF THE DAY TWO PSAE APPLIED MATHEMATICS TEST: The Applied Mathematics Test is 45 minutes long, in which you must answer 33 multiple-choice questions. It is the second test given on the second day of the exam. The test assesses problem-solving skills and critical thinking in mathematics. Figures are not necessarily, but are typically, drawn to scale. The use of a calculator is allowed, and examinees are provided with a formula sheet for the exam.

There are five different levels of questions, ranging from "Level 3" items, which are the least complex, to "Level 7" items, which are the most complex. The questions get progressively more difficult as examinees move through the Applied Mathematics test.

Level 3 items measure skills in performing basic mathematical operations (addition, subtraction, multiplication, and division) and conversions from one form to another, using whole numbers, fractions, decimals, or percentages.

Level 4 questions measure skills in performing one or two mathematical operations, such as addition, subtraction, or multiplication, on several positive or negative numbers.

Level 5 items require test-takers to look up and calculate single-step conversions within English or non-English systems of measurement or between systems of measurement.

Level 6 questions measure test-takers' skills in using negative numbers, fractions, ratios, percentages, and mixed numbers in calculations.

Level 7 items require multiple steps of logic and calculation. Questions may involve more than one unknown, nonlinear functions, and applications of basic statistical concepts.

APPLIED MATHEMATICS GENERAL STRATEGIES: The following are basic general Applied Mathematics strategies:

• *Work as quickly as possible.* The items are arranged in ascending order of difficulty. Therefore, students must be careful not to become bogged down on the earlier problems—otherwise they won't answer enough items to score well. Of course, this does not mean "work fast and make mistakes." Students must strike an appropriate balance between accuracy and speed.

• *Read the question carefully.* It is possible to err by answering the wrong question. The test-writers anticipate this by providing answer choices that match "misinterpreted question stems."

• *Pay careful attention to units.* Students must be very careful in their reading of the question—particularly the units given.

• *Use common sense.* Common sense is a double-punch strategy. First, students should apply common sense to make sure that their own answers make sense. At least two of the answer choices are silly. Second, they can use it as a guessing tool. When a student is running out of time or he or she doesn't know the answer to an item and must

Photocopying not allowed without Cambridge licensing agreement.

- *Don't check your arithmetic.* The test is timed, so students are likely to score highest when they answer as many items as possible, even at the risk of missing a few. Also, a calculation that is done with a calculator does not need to be checked because the computer inside does not make mistakes. Finally, if a student works a problem and gets a result that conforms to one of the five choices, the chances that he or she has made a calculation error are slim to none.

CHECKLIST OF QUESTION-TYPES:

(1) Single-Step Arithmetic

(2) Multi-Step Arithmetic

(3) Average

(4) Percent

(5) Area/Perimeter

(6) Volume

(7) Best Deal

(8) Dimensional Analysis/Mixed Units

(9) Challenge Problems

ADDITIONAL NOTES AND STRATEGIES FROM IN-CLASS DISCUSSION: _____

_____

_____

_____

_____

_____

_____

_____

_____

_____

_____

_____

_____

_____

_____

Day Two PSAE

READING FOR INFORMATION

AMERICA'S #1 STANDARDS-BASED SCHOOL IMPROVEMENT PROGRAM

Cambridge Course Concept Outline
STEP THREE

I. SECTION ONE—READING FOR INFORMATION REVIEW (p. 123)

A. OVERVIEW OF THE READING FOR INFORMATION LESSON

B. INTRODUCTION TO THE READING FOR INFORMATION TEST

C. FORMAT OF THE READING FOR INFORMATION TEST

D. FIVE LEVELS OF QUESTION DIFFICULTY

1. LEVEL 3 QUESTIONS
2. LEVEL 4 QUESTIONS
3. LEVEL 5 QUESTIONS
4. LEVEL 6 QUESTIONS
5. LEVEL 7 QUESTIONS

E. TEST-TAKING STRATEGIES

1. READ THROUGH ENTIRE PASSAGE
2. DON'T TRY TO MEMORIZE DETAILS
3. MARK IMPORTANT POINTS
4. PAY ATTENTION TO UNDERLYING CONCERNS
5. ELIMINATE CHOICES AND GUESS

F. EIGHT MAJOR CATEGORIES OF QUESTIONS

1. MAIN IDEA
2. DETAILS
3. VOCABULARY
4. COMPARATIVE RELATIONSHIPS
5. CAUSE/EFFECT
6. SEQUENCE
7. GENERALIZATIONS
8. AUTHOR'S VOICE

G. READING FOR INFORMATION WALK-THROUGH
(Review Questions #1-10, p. 123)

1. PASSAGE I (p. 123)
   a. CAUSE/EFFECT (Review Questions #1-2, p. 124)

SECTION ONE—READING FOR INFORMATION REVIEW

DIRECTIONS: The questions in this section accompany the in-class review of the Reading for Information concepts and skills tested by the PSAE Reading for Information test. You will work through the questions with your instructor in class. Each passage in this group is followed by questions based on its content. After reading a passage, choose the best answer to each question. Answer all questions following a selection on the basis of what is stated or implied in that passage. Answers are on page 216.

PASSAGE I

State College Athletic Association

Dear Sports Fan:

In order to avoid disappointments such as those of last year and to ensure that the limited seats are fairly allocated, the Athletic Association has adopted a seating lottery for the games during the upcoming football season.

All applications must be postmarked by April 1st to be eligible. Any request postmarked after April 1st will be processed in the order received by the Reserved Seat Office <u>after</u> the original drawing is completed.

A total of 10,000 stadium seats for all home games are available for the general public through the drawing; we expect to receive about 12,000 requests for seats. Before we process the 5,000th application, the Homecoming Game will probably be sold out. The number of seats we are provided by the host school limits the availability of seats for away games.

Seat requests are processed as follows:

Priority 1:   Requests for all ten games of the season—both home and away.
Priority 2:   Requests for all home games for the entire season.
Priority 3:   All other requests.

When we receive your request, we will open the envelope and deposit your check. Depositing your check does not guarantee you seating. On May 1st, the Athletic Association will process each category separately, according to priority, by randomly picking requests. If you do not receive seating, your funds will be returned.

Sincerely,

The Reserved Seat Office
State College Athletic Association

---

1. What may have occurred last year to prompt this letter?

   A. The college's football team had a losing season.
   B. Supporters of visiting teams could not get seats to games.
   C. Fans who didn't get seats felt they were treated unfairly.
   D. Very few graduates returned for the homecoming game.
   E. The Reserved Seat Office received very few seat requests.

2. Applications that are postmarked after April 1st will be

   A. Returned to senders unopened
   B. Eligible only for home games
   C. Handled in order after the lottery
   D. Treated as priority 2 requests
   E. Treated as priority 3 requests

3. According to the letter, the lottery will take place

   A. On April 1st
   B. Between April 2nd and April 30th
   C. On May 1st
   D. After May 1st
   E. Regularly throughout the summer

4. Which of the following requests will receive the most favorable consideration?

   A. One postmarked March 31st for all home games.
   B. One postmarked April 1st for all home games.
   C. One postmarked April 1st for all away games.
   D. One postmarked April 1st for all games.
   E. One postmarked April 2nd for all games.

5. The third paragraph probably mentions the Homecoming Game because

   A. It is the most popular game of the season
   B. More seats are available than for other games
   C. The college team seldom wins that game
   D. More visitors request seats than graduates
   E. Fewer students than graduates request seats

PASSAGE II

Ralph's Corner Deli

MEMO

To: All Delivery Drivers

1. The lunch shift runs from noon until 3:00. The supper shift runs from 5:00 to 9:00. You must arrive 15 minutes prior to the start of your shift.

2. All drivers must wear clean, neat clothing: solid white shirts with collars; black long pants and a belt; white sneakers and white socks. You must wear your official "Ralph's Corner Deli" nametag on the left side of your shirt at the level of the third button on your shirt at all times.

3. If a customer offers you a tip, you may accept it. But you should NEVER ask for a tip. Regardless of whether you have been offered a tip, be sure to thank the customer for doing business with Ralph's Corner Deli.

4. Your car must be inspected and insured. Drive safely and obey all traffic laws. If you receive a traffic ticket while driving, you will be given a warning from Ralph's Corner Deli. If you receive a second ticket within one year, you will be discharged as a driver.

6. What should a driver do if a customer does not offer a tip?

   A. Thank the customer anyway.
   B. Ask for an appropriate tip.
   C. Refuse to deliver the order.
   D. Leave without saying anything.
   E. Stay until a tip is offered.

7. Which of the following must a delivery driver wear?

   A. Dark-colored sneakers
   B. Dark-colored shorts
   C. White T-shirt
   D. Striped dress shirt
   E. White socks

8. What time must a driver arrive to work the supper shift?

   A. 3:15
   B. 4:45
   C. 5:00
   D. 8:45
   E. 9:15

 **Step Three**

PASSAGE III

Maxwell's Gift & Candy Company

To: Shipping Department Personnel
Re: Exporting to Australia

When we start taking orders via the Internet, we expect to ship a number of small parcels to Australia. These may need to be accompanied by paperwork for the Australian import authorities. Refer to the following instructions for guidance.

Australian Quarantine Import Service (AQIS)
A guide to importing biological products and foodstuffs

1. <u>Products requiring an import permit</u>

    Products derived from animals and plants that are:
    • human or animal foods (including dairy products)
    • plant products for livestock feeds
    • agricultural materials
    • food manufacturing materials

2. <u>How to import biological materials and foodstuffs</u>

    You must have a permit application form before you send the goods into the country. For rapid clearance, arrange for a copy of the permit to accompany the goods, either with the person carrying the goods or in an envelope on the side of the parcel. Your goods will be released if all the conditions on the permit have been complied with—but goods that are not accompanied by a permit will be held in quarantine until you can present a valid permit.

3. <u>How to apply for an import permit</u>

    An "Application to Import Quarantine Material" can be obtained from the enquiries officer in the AQIS office in the State or Territory that is the destination of the goods.

    You will be subject to a lodgment charge, as detailed in the application package. The fee is charged according to the complexity of assessing and processing the application. A copy of the fee schedule is also available from the enquiries officer. Your application will not be processed until this fee has been received. Checks should be made payable to: Collector of Public Monies.

    Applications and accompanying fees can be mailed to: Animal Programs Section, AQIS, GPO Box 858, CANBERRA ACT 2601. Alternatively, you can fax your application, together with your credit card details, to (612) 6273 2097.

4. <u>What should be included in the application?</u>

    Many biological materials and foodstuffs are complex products that contain a variety of ingredients. To complete the assessment of your application, AQIS needs to know precisely what these ingredients are, where they come from, and how they have been processed.

5. Where all the necessary information is provided, <u>allow a minimum of three weeks for processing</u>. Complex applications may take longer to assess.

6. <u>Detained goods</u>

    Contact the Detained Goods Officer in the AQIS State office to arrange storage of your goods. If you do not contact the Detained Goods Officer within 30 days of the goods being detained, they will be destroyed.

9. The instructions state that any package you send that is detained and not claimed within 30 days will be

   A. Returned to the sender
   B. Destroyed automatically
   C. Transshipped to quarantine
   D. Forwarded to addressee
   E. Stored indefinitely

10. In this context, the lodgment charge most probably means

   A. Shipping cost
   B. Selling price
   C. Manufacturer's cost
   D. Application refund
   E. Filing fee

11. According to the instructions, a piece of jewelry made of gold and other metals would

   A. Be subject to quarantine pending application processing
   B. Not be covered by the import restrictions set forth
   C. Need to be sent to the purchaser before wearing
   D. Require supporting documentation for each component
   E. Entail a lengthy and complex import application process

12. If you needed to ship a package on a priority basis, which of the following might you do to speed up clearance?

   A. Wait to send all paperwork until AQIS has received the package
   B. Prepay the storage fee for the package during quarantine
   C. Fax the application with a credit card number for the fee
   D. Ship the package directly to the AQIS office in CANBERRA
   E. Send the package without any supporting documentation

NOTES AND STRATEGIES

SECTION TWO—READING FOR INFORMATION PROBLEM-SOLVING

DIRECTIONS: This section contains Reading for Information problems for in-class problem-solving with your instructor. Each passage in this group is followed by questions based on its content. After reading a selection, choose the best answer to each question. Answer all questions following a passage on the basis of what is stated or implied in that passage. Answers are on page 216.

Gooney Bird Airlines

MEMO: TO ALL FLIGHT ATTENDANTS

In the unlikely event that something happens that requires you to land the plane, follow these procedures:

1. If the pilot is unconscious at the controls, push, pull, drag, or carry him or her out of the pilot's seat. (Do not discard the pilot through the exit door as this may pose a threat to persons on the ground.)

2. Assume your position at the controls but don't touch anything just yet. (Especially the red button that says "EJECT!")

3. Put on the radio headset. (If there is no headset, check to make sure that it is not still attached to the pilot—another reason not to discard the pilot.) Use the radio to call for help. There should be a button on the yoke (the plane's steering wheel) or a CB-type microphone on the instrument panel. Depress the button to talk, release to listen. Say "Mayday! Mayday!" and describe your situation giving your destination, plane call numbers (printed on the instrument panel), and a brief description of the problem (*e.g.*, pilot dead, engine on fire, passengers angry over the lack of beverage service in the cabin).

4. If no one answers your "Mayday" call, tune the radio to an easy listening channel and get ready to land the plane yourself. First, familiarize yourself with the controls:

   • *Yoke.* This is the steering wheel and should be directly in front of you. You push forward to descend; pull back to gain altitude; and change direction by turning it to the left or right. The yoke is very sensitive-- move it only an inch or two at a time. While at cruising level, the nose of the plane will be about three inches below the horizon.

   • *Airspeed.* This is on the top of the instrument panel to the left. It is usually calibrated in knots (one knot equals 1-1/4 miles per hour). (No, we don't know why the dial uses knots instead of miles per hour; at least it is not the metric system.)

   • *Throttle.* This is a black lever beside the seat. The throttle controls the airspeed (power). Pull back to cause the plane to slow and descend; push forward to cause the plane to speed up and rise.

   Second, look for a suitable landing site.

   Look first to see whether you can find an airport. (Stay away from O'Hare because last Tuesday's planes are still waiting for clearance to land.) If no airport is nearby, then look for a flat field. (Wheat, oats, and barley are okay; in late summer, corn is a problem.) Don't insist on a perfect landing strip: A bumpy landing is better than crashing. (Almost always.)

   Third, as you approach the landing strip, reduce power. Time your descent so that you are about 100 feet above the landing strip when your airspeed drops to 70 knots. At 60 or 65 knots, the plane will stall and settle to the earth. (Hopefully.) As the plane touches down, pull back all the way on the throttle and use the foot pedal to gently brake, as you would a car.

   Once you have come to a halt, exit the aircraft and move to a safe distance. (Don't forget to remove all company property, including the pilot.)

1. According to the instructions, you will find the plane's call numbers

   A. On the yoke
   B. Inside the radio headset
   C. On the instrument panel
   D. Between the throttle and the seat
   E. In the pilot's coat pocket

2. If you want the plane to gain altitude you should

   A. Use the foot pedals
   B. Turn right or left
   C. Push the throttle forward
   D. Pull the throttle back
   E. Issue instructions on the radio

3. What is the minimum safe airspeed that you must maintain in order to keep the plane in the air?

   A. $1\frac{1}{4}$ knots

   B. 50 knots

   C. 60 knots

   D. 65 knots

   E. 70 knots or more

4. The word "sensitive" as used to describe the yoke means

   A. Emotional
   B. Responsive
   C. Rigid
   D. Unreliable
   E. Weird

5. If the plane's nose appears to be slightly below the horizon, then the plane is

   A. Flying level
   B. Descending
   C. Ascending
   D. On automatic pilot
   E. About to hit the horizon

NOTES AND STRATEGIES

Poe's Pizza Restaurant

INSTRUCTIONS FOR ASSISTANT MANAGERS

When you are scheduled to open the store, you must arrive no later than 9:00 a.m. First, start a batch of dough. The dough will not be ready for the lunch rush unless it has begun to rise by 9:30. Next, check to make sure that the night crew has properly cleaned the kitchen, bathrooms, and eating area. If any area has not been cleaned, you must clean it yourself. If the job takes more than 30 minutes or if there is an emergency, call the Manager at her home. Then you should set up the preparation area. Fill the sauce and all topping containers. Use any time remaining before your break to move stock to the "ready" position in the walk-in cooler. At 11:00, you may take a 15-minute break. After your break, start the oven and set the temperature to 475°F; check and fill napkin dispensers, condiment bottles, and utensil trays in the dining area. When your shift workers arrive at 11:30, have them make five cheese pizzas, three meat pizzas, and two vegetable pizzas. Open the doors for customers at 11:45.

---

6. At what time should the pizza oven be turned on?

   A. 9:30
   B. 10:00
   C. 10:30
   D. 11:15
   E. 12:00

7. If at 9:40 you discover that overnight a pipe has burst in a bathroom, you should:

   A. Attempt to fix it yourself
   B. Call the Manager at her home
   C. Tell the shift workers about it
   D. Close the store for the day
   E. Take your break early

8. When the shift workers arrive, they should be told to make how many pizzas?

   A. 2
   B. 3
   C. 5
   D. 10
   E. 12

SECTION THREE—READING FOR INFORMATION QUIZZES

DIRECTIONS: This section contains three Reading for Information quizzes. Each question is based on the accompanying selection. Complete each quiz while being timed. Answers are on page 216.

QUIZ I (12 questions; 15 minutes)

N O T I C E

Every worker at the shop must insert his/her time card in the time clock before the start of the workday. (8:00 am) Workers who fail to punch in or who punch in late will be docked a full hour of pay.

At the end of the workday (5:00 pm on weekdays, 12:00 noon on Saturdays), everyone must punch out. Workers who punch out before 5:00 pm or who fail to punch out will be docked a full hour of pay.

If you arrive late, you should punch in and then report immediately to your supervisor to explain why you were late. If you must leave before quitting time, you must first notify your supervisor and then punch out.

1. What is the earliest time that a worker can normally punch out during the week?

   A. 7:59 am
   B. 8:00 am
   C. 12:00 noon
   D. 4:59 pm
   E. 5:00 pm

2. According to the notice, a worker who is late should

   A. Go immediately to work and later notify the supervisor
   B. Notify the supervisor and then go punch in
   C. Punch in and then notify the supervisor
   D. Punch in and notify the supervisor after work
   E. Notify the supervisor but not punch in that day

3. If you have to leave work during the day due to personal illness, you should

   A. Leave immediately without punching out but tell your supervisor the next day
   B. Punch out just before you leave and explain the circumstance when you are asked
   C. Punch out when you first begin to feel ill and leave when you have to
   D. Tell your supervisor that you will have to leave work and then leave immediately
   E. Inform your supervisor that you are ill and then punch out before leaving

> **Commonly Asked Questions about Web Courses**
>
> The following information should help you answer inquiries from students who are interested in registering for a web course.
>
> 1. An Internet-based course is designed for flexibility in scheduling work, personal, and school activities. Remember, Internet-based courses are not for everyone. These are independent study courses. Students do a great deal of reading and asking questions by e-mail. There will be fixed times for turning in assignments. Students cannot turn in assignments at any time, such as at the end of the semester. Students who are not comfortable with this method of learning should take traditional courses.
>
> 2. Students can register on campus or by phone. The College phone number is 555-1212.
>
> 3. The web courses begin August 21st and end December 19th. All assignments must be completed and sent to the teacher by December 17th.
>
>   There is a packet of assignments for this course. This packet can be picked up at the bookstore and/or can be mailed to the student. (In order to receive a packet by mail, the student must request one.)
>
> 4. If a student wishes to withdraw from the course, the student must do so three weeks prior to the end of the course. If a student is not keeping up with assignments at the midterm exam, the teacher has the option to withdraw the student from the course. Refer students to the college schedule for midterm exam dates.

4. In paragraph 1, the phrase "traditional courses" means

   A. Classes in which students and teachers meet regularly
   B. Courses that cover basic subject matter
   C. Lessons taught by teachers who are not on campus
   D. Subjects that are usually required in college
   E. Individual tutorial sessions with a teacher

5. Which of the following bits of information must be obtained from another source?

   A. The college phone number
   B. The date courses begin
   C. The date assignments are due
   D. The date for the midterm exam
   E. The date the course ends

6. According to the memo, students are permitted to withdraw from an Internet course

   A. At any time
   B. Within the first three weeks
   C. Up to three weeks before the end
   D. At the midterm exam
   E. Three weeks after the midterm exam

IMPORTANT NOTICE

FROM: County Extension Service
TO: All Farm Workers

Noise from farm tools and machinery can cause permanent hearing loss. Hearing loss may be temporary at first, but repeated exposure will lead to permanent damage. The damage can occur gradually over a number of years and may remain unnoticed until it is too late.

Typical farm noises that can damage hearing include:

- tractor (95-100 decibels)
- header (88-90)
- orchard sprayer (85-100)
- angle grinder (95-105)
- bench grinder (90-95)
- chainsaw (105-120)
- pig shed at feed time (95-105)

The higher the decibels, the more dangerous is the sound.

If you have to shout above workplace noise to be heard by someone a yard away, your hearing could be at risk. If noise cannot be reduced or removed at its source, and there is no other way to separate people from damaging noise exposure, protective hearing equipment must be worn.

You can reduce noise at its source by:

- keeping machinery well maintained; and
- if practicable, running machinery at lower revs.

You can protect yourself from noise exposure by:

- limiting the time you spend in a noisy environment;
- isolating work areas from noisy machinery using distance or insulation;
- scheduling noisy work when fewer workers are around; and
- using job rotation to alternate noisy jobs with quiet ones.

Where noise exposure cannot be reduced, hearing protection should be worn—*e.g.*, on open tractors, or when using a chainsaw.

7. The memo states that hearing loss due to exposure to loud noise

   A. Is always sudden
   B. Can be reversed
   C. May be gradual
   D. Is very painful
   E. Is unavoidable

8. According to the memo, which of the following activities is the noisiest?

   A. Orchard sprayer
   B. Header
   C. Angle grinder
   D. Chainsaw
   E. Pig shed

9. The memo recommends that hearing protection be worn while operating an open tractor because

   A. It is not possible to reduce exposure to the noise
   B. An open tractor poses a serious threat of rollover
   C. Open tractors are much noisier than passenger cars
   D. Open tractors are not usually very well maintained
   E. Workers will have to shout instructions to the operator

Martindale Industries, Inc.

INTERESTED IN APPLYING FOR A POSITION?
HERE ARE SOME THINGS YOU SHOULD KNOW.

ALL position announcements require an official Employment Application form.

TYPE OR PRINT on your application form so that it can be easily read.

COMPLETE each section of the application form with as much relevant information as possible, even if you are also submitting a resume.

DO include: educational background, relevant work experience, special permits/licenses, names of references who can verify your work history, details of your employment that you may not have covered on your application form, names of job-related honors and awards you have received, and other relevant details of employment.

DON'T include: reference to your race, sex, age, religion, ethnic origin, or pictures of yourself.

LETTERS OF RECOMMENDATION should be submitted only when a job announcement specifically requires them. Such letters should be attached to your application packet and should be current.

TRANSCRIPTS should be submitted only when a job announcement specifically requires them. Contact your school for official transcripts as soon as possible. In most circumstances, copies are accepted up until the final interview.

COVER LETTERS are always accepted but usually not required. Letters should be typed and attached to your application materials when they are submitted to the Human Resource Department. The letter should be a statement of your special skills, as well as your interest and motivation for applying for the position. It can also outline the strengths you have and the contribution you would make in the position.

BEST OF LUCK IN YOUR JOB SEARCH!

10. According to the instructions, an application for a job always includes a(n)

    A. Cover letter
    B. Transcript
    C. Picture
    D. Recommendation letter
    E. Application form

11. According to the instructions, personal observations by an applicant about additional qualities would normally be included where?

    A. The application form
    B. A separate cover letter
    C. On the back of a photograph
    D. In a recommendation letter
    E. With an official transcript

12. According to the instructions, it would not be acceptable to

    A. Substitute a resume for a completed application form
    B. Provide a transcript (if required) before the interview
    C. Include the names of reference to verify information
    D. Attach a cover letter to the other application materials
    E. Submit an application to the Human Resource Department

QUIZ II (10 questions; 15 minutes)

MEMO

RE: New Parking Regulations

The company parking lot has recently been repainted so that colored lines indicate the type of parking available. The 12 parking spaces immediately outside the main entrance are lined in green, and signs indicate that these are reserved for visitors. The 15 parking spaces to the right of the building are lined in red and are reserved for management. The parking area behind the building is lined in blue and is for all other uses.

1. An employee who is not management should park in

   A. A green space immediately outside the main entrance
   B. A red space to the right of the building
   C. A blue space behind the building
   D. Either a green space or a blue space
   E. Either a blue space or a red space

Smithtown Pets

To: All Sales Employees
Subject: AKC Registrations for New Puppies

An unscrupulous dog breeder in our area has been telling prospective buyers that a puppy is "show quality" hoping that the customer will mistakenly believe that it is eligible for AKC registration when it is not. You need to make clear to our customers the difference.

AKC stands for American Kennel Club, a not-for-profit organization of dog owners that was established in 1884 and maintains a purebred dog registry. In order for a puppy to be registered with the AKC, the sire (father) and dam (mother) must have been registered. Then, when a litter of puppies is whelped, the litter must also be registered. At that point, each individual puppy in the litter can be registered if the owner chooses.

An "AKC" registration certificate only identifies the dog as the offspring of a known sire and dam, born on a known date. It doesn't indicate the quality of the animal or its state of health. Quality, in the sense of "show quality," is determined by many factors including health, physical conformation, ability to move, and general appearance.

Some of the puppies we sell are purebred; others are not. If a puppy is purebred, then we have the AKC registration and will deliver it with the puppy at the time of sale. The customer must understand, however, that an AKC registered puppy may or may not grow up to be a show dog. We also sell non-purebred puppies. These cannot be registered, but they make fine pets.

2. As used in the first sentence, "unscrupulous" means

   A. Successful
   B. Dishonest
   C. Courageous
   D. Temporary
   E. Ineligible

3. Management probably wrote this memo in response to

   A. Customer complaints about the service at Smithtown Pets
   B. An announcement by the AKC of new registration procedures
   C. Lost sales due to confusion about AKC registration and quality
   D. The establishment of the American Kennel Club's registry
   E. Some letters from potential customers outside the area

4. Based on the passage, if the sire and dam of a litter of puppies are registered with the AKC, then the puppies in the litter are

   A. Automatically registered with the AKC
   B. Probably not going to be good pets
   C. Certainly going to be healthy
   D. More likely to be show quality than not
   E. Eligible for registration with the AKC

MARKETING SURVEY
TELEPHONE INTERVIEWING INSTRUCTIONS

Ask the questions set forth in *italics*. Enter the responses using your computer keyboard.

All numeric fields must be stored as right justified. All character fields must be stored as left justified.

1. *What is your address where you live or stay most of the time?*

- *What is the house number?*
  Enter the house number. (Max. of 6 characters.)

- *What is the road or street?*
  Enter the road or street. (Max. of 14 characters.)

- *Do you have an apartment number?*
  Enter the apartment number. (Max. of 6 characters.)

NOTE: If the respondent gives a post office box say:

The address that you provided contained a box number. It is preferable for us to have a street or road name with a house number.

If the respondent provides a house number, enter as shown above. If the respondent does not provide a house number, mark "N" for "No House Number."

2. *What are the names of all persons living or staying at this address, starting please with the person who owns, is buying, or rents this house or apartment?*

Enter as many names as you are given, starting with the last name, then the first name and any middle initial.

After you have recorded the names, then for each name ask:

- *How are you related to...?* [Use the name of the person.]

Enter one of the following:

S ↔ SPOUSE

O ↔ OTHER
(Other member of immediate family)

R ↔ ROOMER
(Includes boarder, roommate, housemate, *etc.*)

3. *What is the total annual income of your household?*

A ↔ below $10,000

B ↔ $10,001—$20,000

C ↔ $20,001—$30,000

---

5. If you ask you first question and the respondent gives a post office box, you should

A. Enter the number up to 6 characters
B. Enter the number up to 14 characters
C. Ask again for a house number
D. Enter the letter "N"
E. Ask for an apartment number

6. In question two, the "name of the person" refers to the

A. Name of the caller
B. First name of the respondent
C. Last name of the respondent
D. Names of persons other than the respondent
E. Name of all persons living at the address

7. Which of the following information must be stored as right justified?

A. House number
B. Spouse's name
C. Annual income information
D. "No house number" entry
E. Relationship status

Compuporium

Store Guarantee

Compuporium offers a limited money back guarantee for thirty (30) days on new Products and five (5) days on remanufactured Products. To receive a refund under the limited money back guarantee, you must notify Compuporium of your desire to return the Product within thirty (30) days or five (5) days, as applicable, from the date you received your Product. You must also return the Product and all accessories to Compuporium within seven (7) days after you receive a return merchandise authorization ("RMA") kit and otherwise follow the procedures described below.

1. Compuporium will refund the original purchase price of the Product and applicable sales tax. Shipping, handling, and insurance (including applicable sales taxes) that you paid when you bought your Product are not refundable.

2. Contact Compuporium with your system serial number and order number. We will provide you with an RMA kit that will include an RMA number, authorize the return of your Product, and provide other instructions.

3. Ship the Product to the appropriate addresses printed on the labels contained in the RMA kit using the original boxes and packing materials. Write the RMA number in large, clear characters on the outside of each box that you ship. You must include a copy of your packing slip with the returned Product to establish proof of purchase. You must also return all disks, cables, and manuals supplied with the Product.

4. The returned Product must be in the same condition as you received it. You must return all pre-loaded software with the Product to obtain a refund for the Product, and you may only return pre-loaded software if you choose to return the Product. You may return other software only if the package has not been opened.

5. Upon receipt, Compuporium will inspect the Product and, after accepting it, process your request for a refund within seven (7) business days. Compuporium will notify you if your Product and Accessories are not accepted.

8. The phrase "including applicable sales taxes" used in the parentheses in item one refers to

   A. All sales tax paid on the original purchase price for the product
   B. The cost of shipping and handling the product and cost of insurance
   C. Additional sales tax on shipping, handling, and insurance
   D. Money that will be refunded only if the product is accepted by Compuporium
   E. Charges assessed by the government for returning merchandise

9. A customer can find the RMA number

   A. On the box of the original system
   B. In the guarantee for the system
   C. With the serial number on the system
   D. In the kit supplied by Compuporium
   E. With the cables and other accessories

10. According to the terms of the guarantee, any software installed by a customer after receiving a system

   A. Must be uninstalled before it is returned to Compuporium
   B. Becomes the property of Compuporium when the system is returned
   C. Is subject to sales tax according to applicable law
   D. Is covered by the guarantee only if it has not been opened
   E. Requires prior approval before it can be returned to the store

QUIZ III (11 questions; 15 minutes)

ACME Delivery Company

When driving a company van, pay attention to the indicators on the dashboard. If the "SERVICE ENGINE" light comes on, you have engine trouble.

If the light stays lit, then you can continue your deliveries. When you return to the warehouse, tell the Dispatcher about the problem when you return the keys. If the light begins to flash, pull over to the side of the road as soon as you can do so safely. Turn on the truck's emergency flashers and contact the Dispatcher by two-way radio. Wait for a company mechanic to arrive. Do not leave the truck.

---

1. According to the passage, the first thing you must do if the "SERVICE ENGINE" light begins to flash is

   A. Contact the dispatcher
   B. Return the keys
   C. Continue deliveries
   D. Pull off the road
   E. Use the radio

2. If you have trouble that forces you to suspend deliveries, after you have contacted the office you should

   A. Search the immediate neighborhood for a mechanic who can make repairs
   B. Find a comfortable place such as a diner to wait for the company mechanic
   C. Stay with the truck until the company mechanics comes to make repairs
   D. Walk to the nearest payphone to telephone customers that the deliveries will be late
   E. Find alternative transportation and return to the warehouse as soon as possible

To All Employees Who Do Vehicle Inspections
Please READ the Attached Memo

DIVISION OF AIR RESOURCES BUREAU OF ENHANCED INSPECTION AND MAINTENANCE
State's New Auto Emission Inspection/Maintenance Program

The State's new auto emission program is a federally required program that ensures vehicles are inspected and properly maintained to minimize pollution. The program requires two separate types of tests: one for vehicle owners in Major Metropolitan Areas (MMA) and one for vehicle owners throughout the rest of the state. The new testing, which begins next year, is required to improve air quality to meet federal standards. Emission tests will be required annually, in addition to the current safety inspection.

NON-MMA COUNTIES

Vehicle owners in the non-MMA counties will now be required to have their cars inspected for vehicle emissions. The new test consists of an annual gas-cap check, an anti-tampering visual inspection, and an on-board diagnostic (OBD) check on 1996 and newer vehicles. The test will be performed at the same time as the annual safety inspection and/or with a change of vehicle ownership. Licensed test and repair facilities will perform the inspections.

MMA COUNTIES

The emissions testing program has been upgraded to meet federal requirements. Vehicles registered in an MMA will now be required to pass a more stringent emission inspection.

Emissions tests will be performed at the same licensed test-and-repair inspection facilities where safety inspections are performed. The tests will be required annually and/or when a change of vehicle ownership occurs.

An OBD check on model year 1996 or newer vehicles and an anti-tampering visual inspection of the air pollution control devices will be performed.

Model year 1981 (or newer vehicles having a gross vehicle weight of 8,500 pounds or less) will be checked for gas leaks and excessive emissions with special equipment purchased by the inspection station owner.

Vehicles before model year 1981 and gas-powered vehicles over 8,500 lbs. will undergo a more lenient test for emissions.

Vehicles less than two years old, diesels, electric vehicles, and those with historic or farm equipment registration are exempt.

Test results will be sent electronically to the Department of Motor Vehicles. Failed vehicles may be repaired at the same facility.

3. According to the memo, for vehicles registered in a non-MMA county

   A. A new emissions test will be required
   B. The old emissions test has been upgraded
   C. A new safety inspection test is being implemented
   D. Some new cars will not have to be inspected
   E. Older cars cannot pass the safety inspection

4. According to the memo, when a person buys a previously owned car, the

   A. Vehicle must be reinspected
   B. Previous inspection is good for a year
   C. Previous inspection is good until the annual registration renewal
   D. Previous inspection is good until the next annual inspection
   E. Vehicle need not have an emissions test

5. According to the memo, a model year 1980 vehicle is

   A. Subject to a stricter emissions test
   B. Subject to a more lenient emissions test
   C. Not required to be tested for emissions
   D. To be given an old test for emissions
   E. To be examined visually for emissions compliance

Leo's Professional Photography

To: All Office Staff
Re: How to Answer Telephone Inquiries Regarding Wedding Photography

1.   How much will it cost?
When a potential client asks about cost, explain that we do not give estimates over the telephone. You can, however, say that couples typically budget about $1,500 for photography. Emphasize that in this field, perhaps more than any other, you usually get what you pay for. Encourage the potential client to make an appointment to visit our studio. There is no fee for a consultation.

2.   What quality of pictures do we produce?
Explain that we use <u>medium format</u> (as opposed to 35mm) for the important events of the day because medium format cameras provide a larger negative. (For candid photos, our photographers do use 35mm cameras.) The main advantage of the medium format is better color saturation of the negative—which means a better quality print.

Emphasize that our photographers always bring backup equipment in case of an emergency. Also, we use <u>double lighting</u> and <u>soft focus</u> techniques for that professional touch.

3.   What type of album do we provide?
The brand is Artistic Leather, the best available. It is guaranteed for life. Mention that they can choose from several different finishes. If the caller seems worried about cost, then say that we also offer Royalhyde which looks, feels, and wears like leather, but costs much less money.

4.   Who will take the pictures?
First, say that every member of our staff is a highly qualified professional. Then ask if the caller has seen the work of a particular member of our staff. If so, then tell them that you can have the photographer available for a consultation if they wish to come to the studio. We will make every effort to schedule the photographer of their choice.

5.   Can we hold a particular date open?
We cannot book dates over the phone. Again, encourage the caller to make an appointment for an in-studio consultation.

6. If a caller asks about cost, you should first:

   A. Give them an estimate of $1500 for wedding photography
   B. Explain that all work is of the highest quality
   C. Ask them what date they have scheduled their wedding
   D. Tell them about the various techniques that are used
   E. Say that the studio does not give telephone estimates

7. Overall, the answers you give to the questions are designed to encourage the customer to

   A. Make a reservation over the telephone
   B. Ask for a particular photographer by name
   C. Schedule an in-studio consultation
   D. Choose the type of album to be used
   E. Call back at a later time for more information

8. The passage indicates that "double lighting" and "soft focus" are

   A. Pieces of photograph equipment
   B. Photographic techniques
   C. Poses used for wedding photographs
   D. Methods for storing important photos
   E. Types of photographic albums

AllStar Paving

PROCEDURES FOR SMALL CONCRETE JOBS

1. Determine How Much Concrete You'll Need to Mix

The following is a table giving the number of cubic yards of concrete required to pour slabs of different size and thickness. To use this table, multiply the length by the width of the area you plan to concrete. This will give you the square footage in the area.

Area in Square Feet	Thickness in Inches				
	4	5	6	8	12
50	0.62	0.77	0.93	1.2	1.9
100	1.2	1.5	1.9	2.5	3.7
200	2.5	3.1	3.7	4.9	7.4
300	3.7	4.7	5.6	7.4	11.1
400	4.9	6.2	7.4	9.8	14.8
500	6.2	7.2	9.3	12.4	18.6

Cubic Yards of Concrete in Slabs of Various Thickness

Refer to the number of square feet and the thickness in inches of the slab you plan to pour. The figures on the appropriate line will show the number of cubic yards of concrete required to do the job.

2. Mix the Concrete

There are four basic elements in any concrete: Portland cement, fine aggregate such as sand, coarse aggregate such as crushed rock or gravel, and water. The aggregates (sand and gravel) usually make up from 2/3 to 3/4 of the volume of any finished concrete.

For retaining walls, about 6-1/4 gallons of water will be used for each sack of cement if the sand is damp. However, if the sand is wet, 5-1/2 gallons of water will easily do the job. Concrete mixed for pouring sidewalks, stepping stones, slabs, *etc.* will require about 5-3/4 gallons of water per sack of cement if the sand is damp, approximately 5 gallons of water if the sand is wet. If you are pouring sidewalks, steps, *etc.* use 1 part Portland cement to 2 parts sand and 3 parts gravel.

3. Pour the Concrete

Lightly spray the entire area within the form with a garden hose and pour in the concrete. After the form is filled, tamp the freshly poured concrete to compact it. After the concrete in the form has been thoroughly tamped, use a straight edged 2 x 4 as a screed for leveling the concrete. Work the 2 x 4 back and forth, in saw fashion, to level the concrete at all points.

4. Keep the Concrete Moist

Hose down the concrete with a fine mist every hour until you leave the job site.

9. According to the table provided, a slab with an area of 200 square feet and a thickness of 6 inches requires how many cubic yards of concrete?

   A. 1.9
   B. 3.7
   C. 4.9
   D. 6.2
   E. 7.4

10. How many gallons of water should be used per sack of cement to mix concrete for stepping-stones if the sand is wet?

   A. 2
   B. 3
   C. 5
   D. 5-3/4
   E. 6-1/4

11. "Screed" is a technique used to

   A. Mix concrete
   B. Level concrete
   C. Tamp concrete
   D. Moisten concrete
   E. Measure concrete

CAMBRIDGE
EDUCATIONAL SERVICES®
C

AMERICA'S #1 STANDARDS-BASED SCHOOL IMPROVEMENT PROGRAM

Strategy Summary Sheet
Day Two PSAE—Reading for Information

STRUCTURE OF THE DAY TWO PSAE READING FOR INFORMATION TEST: The Reading for Information test is 45 minutes long with 33 multiple-choice questions. The test includes approximately 15 reading samples that range in length from about 50 to 300 words, followed by one, two, or three multiple-choice questions for each sample. It is the third and final test given on the second day of the exam. The test is designed to assess one's skills in reading and using work-related information, including instructions, policies, memos, bulletins, notices, letters, manuals, and governmental regulations.

There are five different levels of questions, ranging from "Level 3" items, which are the least complex, to "Level 7" items, which are the most complex. The questions get progressively more difficult as examinees move through the Reading for Information test.

Level 3 items measure skills in reading short, uncomplicated passages that use elementary vocabulary. The reading materials include basic company policies, procedures, and announcements.

At Level 4, the passages are slightly more complex than those at Level 3. They contain more detail and describe procedures that involve a greater number of steps.

Level 5 passages are more detailed, more complicated, and cover broader topics than those at Level 4. Words and phrases may be specialized (*e.g.*, jargon and technical terms), and some words may have multiple meanings.

Level 6 passages are significantly more difficult than those at the previous level. The presentation of the information is more complex; passages may include excerpts from regulatory and legal documents.

Level 7 questions are similar to those at Level 6 in that they require the examinee to generalize beyond the stated situation, to recognize implied details, and to recognize the probable rationale behind policies and procedures.

READING FOR INFORMATION GENERAL STRATEGIES: The following are basic general Reading for Information strategies:

- *Read through the entire passage.* The first thing that students should do is read through the entire passage to get an overall understanding of the information.

- *Don't try to memorize details.* There simply isn't time to memorize, nor is there any need to do so. After all, this is an open book test.

- *Mark important points.* Students do not have to memorize anything, but they do have to find information. Students should be alert for important points and are encouraged to star or circle such points.

- *Pay attention to underlying concerns.* Often, a question can be answered by reference to underlying concerns or overriding goals.

- *Eliminate choices and guess.* As always, it is important to eliminate any implausible choices and choose from

CHECKLIST OF QUESTION-TYPES:

(1) Main Idea

(2) Details

(3) Vocabulary

(4) Comparative Relationships

(5) Cause/Effect

(6) Sequence

(7) Generalizations

(8) Author's Voice

ADDITIONAL NOTES AND STRATEGIES FROM IN-CLASS DISCUSSION: _____

_____

_____

_____

_____

_____

_____

_____

_____

_____

_____

_____

_____

_____

_____

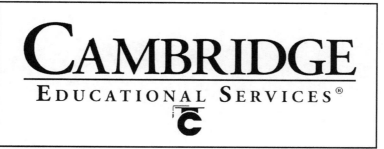

Day Two PSAE

STEP FOUR: PRACTICE TEST REINFORCEMENT

AMERICA'S #1 STANDARDS-BASED SCHOOL IMPROVEMENT PROGRAM

Cambridge Course Concept Outline
STEP FOUR

CAMBRIDGE
EDUCATIONAL SERVICES®

AMERICA'S #1 STANDARDS-BASED SCHOOL IMPROVEMENT PROGRAM

Student Instructions for Step Four: Practice Test Reinforcement

With Step Four: Practice Test Reinforcement, you will need to practice everything that you've learned up to this point in the PSAE course. The practice tests will prepare you for the actual test day and allow you to comfortably try out all the new skills and test-taking strategies that you learned in class. Be sure to complete all four of these practice tests—two with time restrictions and two without time restrictions. Practicing with time limits forces you to adapt your test-taking routine to the stringent time restrictions that are enforced on the real test and to perform to the best of your ability under actual test conditions. Practicing without time limits allows you to focus on the content of the test problems and how to solve problems correctly and more efficiently.

You will find four full-length ACT Practice Tests in the *Cambridge ACT • PLAN • EXPLORE Victory Student Textbook* and additional Day Two PSAE practice material online at the following Website: **www.isbe.net/assessment/psae.htm**. Here, you can download sample problems and also go through online practice problems.

The Step Four progress reports that are included in this chapter allow you to track your performance on the four ACT Practice Tests that are located in the *Cambridge ACT • PLAN • EXPLORE Victory Student Textbook*. Complete the student copy for your own reference and then complete the instructor copy to submit to your teacher.

ACT SCIENCE REASONING
STEP FOUR PROGRESS REPORT
(Student Copy)

The Step Four Progress Reports are designed to help you monitor your ACT Practice Test progress.

DIRECTIONS: Complete the assigned problems, correct your answers, and record both the number and percentage of problems that you answered correctly. Identify the date on which you completed each section of the tests. Your teacher will instruct you on whether additional review problems are necessary.

Transfer this information to the Instructor Copy, and then give that report to your instructor.

Name _____ Student ID _____ Date _____

ACT SCIENCE REASONING PRACTICE TESTS
(Student Copy)

ACT Science Reasoning Practice Test	Total #		# Correct	% Correct	Date Completed	Problem #s to Review
	Possible	Assigned				
1. Practice Test I	40					
2. Practice Test II	40					
3. Practice Test III	40					
4. Practice Test IV	40					

ACT SCIENCE REASONING
STEP FOUR PROGRESS REPORT
(Instructor Copy)

The Step Four Progress Reports are designed to help you monitor your ACT Practice Test progress.

DIRECTIONS: Transfer the information from your Student Copy to the Instructor Copy below. Leave the last three bolded columns blank. Your instructor will use them to evaluate your progress. When finished, give this report to your instructor.

Name _____ Student ID _____ Date _____

ACT SCIENCE REASONING PRACTICE TESTS
(Instructor Copy)

ACT Science Reasoning Practice Test	Total # Possible	Assigned	# Correct	% Correct	Date Completed	Problem #s to Review	Instructor Skill Evaluation (Check One Per Exercise) Mastered	Partially Mastered	Not Mastered
1. Practice Test I	40								
2. Practice Test II	40								
3. Practice Test III	40								
4. Practice Test IV	40								

ACT MATHEMATICS
STEP FOUR PROGRESS REPORT
(Student Copy)

The Step Four Progress Reports are designed to help you monitor your ACT Practice Test progress.

DIRECTIONS: Complete the assigned problems, correct your answers, and record both the number and percentage of problems that you answered correctly. Identify the date on which you completed each section of the tests. Your teacher will instruct you on whether additional review problems are necessary.

Transfer this information to the Instructor Copy, and then give that report to your instructor.

Name _____ Student ID _____ Date _____

ACT MATHEMATICS PRACTICE TESTS
(Student Copy)

ACT Mathematics Practice Test	Total # Possible	Assigned	# Correct	% Correct	Date Completed	Problem #s to Review
1. Practice Test I	60					
2. Practice Test II	60					
3. Practice Test III	60					
4. Practice Test IV	60					

ACT MATHEMATICS
STEP FOUR PROGRESS REPORT
(Instructor Copy)

The Step Four Progress Reports are designed to help you monitor your ACT Practice Test progress.

DIRECTIONS: Transfer the information from your Student Copy to the Instructor Copy below. Leave the last three bolded columns blank. Your instructor will use them to evaluate your progress. When finished, give this report to your instructor.

Name _____ Student ID _____ Date _____

ACT MATHEMATICS PRACTICE TESTS
(Instructor Copy)

ACT Mathematics Practice Test	Total # Possible	Assigned	# Correct	% Correct	Date Completed	Problem #s to Review	Instructor Skill Evaluation (Check One Per Exercise) Mastered	Partially Mastered	Not Mastered
1. Practice Test I	60								
2. Practice Test II	60								
3. Practice Test III	60								
4. Practice Test IV	60								

ACT READING
STEP FOUR PROGRESS REPORT
(Student Copy)

The Step Four Progress Reports are designed to help you monitor your ACT Practice Test progress.

DIRECTIONS: Complete the assigned problems, correct your answers, and record both the number and percentage of problems that you answered correctly. Identify the date on which you completed each section of the tests. Your teacher will instruct you on whether additional review problems are necessary.

Transfer this information to the Instructor Copy, and then give that report to your instructor.

Name _____ Student ID _____ Date _____

ACT READING PRACTICE TESTS
(Student Copy)

ACT Reading Practice Test	Total # Possible	Assigned	# Correct	% Correct	Date Completed	Problem #s to Review
1. Practice Test I	40					
2. Practice Test II	40					
3. Practice Test III	40					
4. Practice Test IV	40					

ACT READING
STEP FOUR PROGRESS REPORT
(Instructor Copy)

The Step Four Progress Reports are designed to help you monitor your ACT Practice Test progress.

DIRECTIONS: Transfer the information from your Student Copy to the Instructor Copy below. Leave the last three bolded columns blank. Your instructor will use them to evaluate your progress. When finished, give this report to your instructor.

Name _____ Student ID _____ Date _____

ACT READING PRACTICE TESTS
(Instructor Copy)

ACT Reading Practice Test	Total #		# Correct	% Correct	Date Completed	Problem #s to Review	Instructor Skill Evaluation (Check One Per Exercise)		
	Possible	Assigned					Mastered	Partially Mastered	Not Mastered
1. Practice Test I	40								
2. Practice Test II	40								
3. Practice Test III	40								
4. Practice Test IV	40								

ACT ENGLISH
STEP FOUR PROGRESS REPORT
(Student Copy)

The Step Four Progress Reports are designed to help you monitor your ACT Practice Test progress.

DIRECTIONS: Complete the assigned problems, correct your answers, and record both the number and percentage of problems that you answered correctly. Identify the date on which you completed each section of the tests. Your teacher will instruct you on whether additional review problems are necessary.

Transfer this information to the Instructor Copy, and then give that report to your instructor.

Name _____ Student ID _____ Date _____

ACT ENGLISH PRACTICE TESTS
(Student Copy)

ACT English Practice Test	Total # Possible	Total # Assigned	# Correct	% Correct	Date Completed	Problem #s to Review
1. Practice Test I	75					
2. Practice Test II	75					
3. Practice Test III	75					
4. Practice Test IV	75					

ACT ENGLISH
STEP FOUR PROGRESS REPORT
(Instructor Copy)

The Step Four Progress Reports are designed to help you monitor your ACT Practice Test progress.

DIRECTIONS: Transfer the information from your Student Copy to the Instructor Copy below. Leave the last three bolded columns blank. Your instructor will use them to evaluate your progress. When finished, give this report to your instructor.

Student Name _____ Student ID _____ Date _____

ACT ENGLISH PRACTICE TESTS
(Instructor Copy)

ACT English Practice Test	Total #						Instructor Skill Evaluation (Check One Per Section)		
	Possible	Assigned	# Correct	% Correct	Date Completed	Problem #s to Review	Mastered	Partially Mastered	Not Mastered
1. Practice Test I	75								
2. Practice Test II	75								
3. Practice Test III	75								
4. Practice Test IV	75								

STEP FIVE: STANDARDS-BASED POST-ASSESSMENT, REPORT, AND REVIEW

Day Two PSAE

STEP FIVE: STANDARDS-BASED POST-ASSESSMENT, REPORT, AND REVIEW

AMERICA'S #1 STANDARDS-BASED SCHOOL IMPROVEMENT PROGRAM

Cambridge Course Concept Outline
STEP FIVE

I. DAY TWO PSAE MIRROR POST-TEST PROGRESS REPORTS
(p. 183)

II. DAY TWO PSAE MIRROR POST-TEST BUBBLE SHEET

DAY TWO PSAE
MIRROR POST-TEST PROGRESS REPORT
(Student Copy)

The Mirror Post-Test Progress Reports are designed to help you make sense of your Day Two PSAE Mirror Post-Test results. Your instructor will use this information to help you make a study plan for topics to study between now and the date of the exam.

DIRECTIONS: Complete the diagnostic post-test and record both the number and percentage of problems that you answered correctly. Identify the date on which you completed each section of the post-test and list the numbers of any problems that you would like your instructor to review in class. If you are using the Cambridge Assessment Service, consult your PSAE Error Analysis for a breakdown of problems by category to complete the remainder of the form. Rank your weakest areas by category so that your instructor will know which areas to target when helping you to design your study plan.

Transfer this information to the Instructor Copy, and then give that report to your instructor.

Name _____ Student ID _____ Date _____

ISBE-Developed Science
(Student Copy)

Date Completed: _____ Total # Possible: 45   # Correct: _____   % Correct: _____

Question Category	Total # Possible	# Correct	% Correct	Problem #s to Review	Rank
Biology					
Chemistry					
Earth					
Ecology					
Physics					
Society					
Space					

DAY TWO PSAE
MIRROR POST-TEST PROGRESS REPORT
(Instructor Copy)

The Mirror Post-Test Progress Reports are designed to help you make sense of your Day Two PSAE Mirror Post-Test results. Your instructor will use this information to help you make a study plan for topics to study between now and the date of the exam.

DIRECTIONS: Transfer the information from your Student Copy to the Instructor Copy below. Your instructor will use the last two bolded columns to evaluate your progress. Leave them blank. When finished, give this report to your instructor.

Name _____ Student ID _____ Date _____

ISBE-Developed Science
(Instructor Copy)

Date Completed: _____ Total # Possible: 45 # Correct: _____ % Correct: _____

Question Category	Total # Possible	# Correct	% Correct	Problem #s to Review	Rank	Instructor Skill Evaluation	
						Review Needed? (Y or N)	Review Section and Problem Numbers Assigned
Biology							
Chemistry							
Earth							
Ecology							
Physics							
Society							
Space							

DAY TWO PSAE
MIRROR POST-TEST PROGRESS REPORT
(Student Copy)

The Mirror Post-Test Progress Reports are designed to help you make sense of your Day Two PSAE Mirror Post-Test results. Your instructor will use this information to help you make a study plan for topics to study between now and the date of the exam.

DIRECTIONS: Complete the diagnostic post-test and record both the number and percentage of problems that you answered correctly. Identify the date on which you completed each section of the post-test and list the numbers of any problems that you would like your instructor to review in class. If you are using the Cambridge Assessment Service, consult your PSAE Error Analysis for a breakdown of problems by category to complete the remainder of the form. Rank your weakest areas by category so that your instructor will know which areas to target when helping you to design your study plan.

Transfer this information to the Instructor Copy, and then give that report to your instructor.

Name _____ Student ID _____ Date _____

Applied Mathematics
(Student Copy)

Date Completed: _____   Total # Possible: 33   # Correct: _____   % Correct: _____

Question Category	Total # Possible	# Correct	% Correct	Problem #s to Review	Rank
Multi-Step Area/Perimeter					
Multi-Step Averages					
Multi-Step Best Deal					
Multi-Step Dimensional Analysis					
Multi-Step Mixed Units					
Multi-Step Rates					
Multi-Step Volumes					
Single-Step Area/Perimeter					
Single-Step Arithmetic					
Single-Step Averages					
Single-Step Best Deal					
Single-Step Dimensional Analysis					
Single-Step Mixed Units					
Single-Step Percent					

DAY TWO PSAE
MIRROR POST-TEST PROGRESS REPORT

(Instructor Copy)

The Mirror Post-Test Progress Reports are designed to help you make sense of your Day Two PSAE Mirror Post-Test results. Your instructor will use this information to help you make a study plan for topics to study between now and the date of the exam.

DIRECTIONS: Transfer the information from your Student Copy to the Instructor Copy below. Your instructor will use the last two bolded columns to evaluate your progress. Leave them blank. When finished, give this report to your instructor.

Name ______________________ Student ID ____________ Date ____________

Applied Mathematics

(Instructor Copy)

Date Completed: ______________ Total # Possible: 33 # Correct: _______ % Correct: _______

Question Category	*Total # Possible*	*# Correct*	*% Correct*	*Problem #s to Review*	*Rank*	**Instructor Skill Evaluation** *Review Needed? (Y or N)*	*Review Section and Problem Numbers Assigned*
Multi-Step Area/Perimeter							
Multi-Step Averages							
Multi-Step Best Deal							
Multi-Step Dimensional Analysis							
Multi-Step Mixed Units							
Multi-Step Rates							
Multi-Step Volumes							
Single-Step Area/Perimeter							
Single-Step Arithmetic							
Single-Step Averages							
Single-Step Best Deal							
Single-Step Dimensional Analysis							
Single-Step Mixed Units							
Single-Step Percent							

DAY TWO PSAE
MIRROR POST-TEST PROGRESS REPORT
(Student Copy)

The Mirror Post-Test Progress Reports are designed to help you make sense of your Day Two PSAE Mirror Post-Test results. Your instructor will use this information to help you make a study plan for topics to study between now and the date of the exam.

DIRECTIONS: Complete the diagnostic post-test and record both the number and percentage of problems that you answered correctly. Identify the date on which you completed each section of the post-test and list the numbers of any problems that you would like your instructor to review in class. If you are using the Cambridge Assessment Service, consult your PSAE Error Analysis for a breakdown of problems by category to complete the remainder of the form. Rank your weakest areas by category so that your instructor will know which areas to target when helping you to design your study plan.

Transfer this information to the Instructor Copy, and then give that report to your instructor.

Name _____ Student ID _____ Date _____

Reading for Information
(Student Copy)

Date Completed: _____ Total # Possible: 33   # Correct: _____   % Correct: _____

Question Category	Total # Possible	# Correct	% Correct	Problem #s to Review	Rank
Author's Voice					
Cause/Effect					
Comparative Relationships					
Details					
Generalizations					
Main Idea					
Sequence					
Vocabulary					

DAY TWO PSAE
MIRROR POST-TEST PROGRESS REPORT
(Instructor Copy)

The Mirror Post-Test Progress Reports are designed to help you make sense of your Day Two PSAE Mirror Post-Test results. Your instructor will use this information to help you make a study plan for topics to study between now and the date of the exam.

DIRECTIONS: Transfer the information from your Student Copy to the Instructor Copy below. Your instructor will use the last two bolded columns to evaluate your progress. Leave them blank. When finished, give this report to your instructor.

Name _____ Student ID _____ Date _____

Reading for Information
(Instructor Copy)

Date Completed: _____ Total # Possible: 33   # Correct: _____   % Correct: _____

Question Category	Total # Possible	# Correct	% Correct	Problem #s to Review	Rank	Review Needed? (Y or N)	Review Section and Problem Numbers Assigned
Author's Voice							
Cause/Effect							
Comparative Relationships							
Details							
Generalizations							
Main Idea							
Sequence							
Vocabulary							

Day Two PSAE Mirror Post-Test Bubble Sheet

Name ___   **Student ID Number** ___

Date ___   **Instructor** ___   **Course/Session Number** ___

USE THIS BUBBLE SHEET ONLY IF YOU ARE NOT USING THE CAMBRIDGE ASSESSMENT REPORT SERVICE

MARK ONE AND ONLY ONE ANSWER TO EACH QUESTION. BE SURE TO COMPLETELY FILL IN THE SPACE FOR YOUR INTENDED ANSWER CHOICE. IF YOU ERASE, DO SO COMPLETELY. MAKE NO STRAY MARKS.

1 ISBE-Developed Science (1–48, A B C D / F G H J)

2 Applied Mathematics (1–36, A B C D E / F G H J K)

3 Reading for Information (1–36, A B C D E / F G H J K)

Photocopying not allowed without Cambridge licensing agreement.   –195–

STEP SIX: PERSONAL STUDY PLAN

Day Two PSAE

STEP SIX: PERSONAL STUDY PLAN

AMERICA'S #1 STANDARDS-BASED SCHOOL IMPROVEMENT PROGRAM

Cambridge Course Concept Outline
STEP SIX

AMERICA'S #1 STANDARDS-BASED SCHOOL IMPROVEMENT PROGRAM

Student Instructions for Step Six: Personal Study Plan

Now that you've reached Step Six of the *Cambridge Day Two PSAE Victory Student Textbook*, you're at the conclusion of your PSAE course. But you're not done yet. You still need to review your overall performance throughout the course, especially focusing on your weakest areas that are indicated on your Day One (ACT) and Day Two PSAE post-tests.

Included in this chapter are Step Six: Personal Study Plan progress reports. These reports allow you to compare your performance on both the Day One (ACT) and Day Two PSAE post-tests, as well as to identify your weakest content areas. With this information, you can then try to eliminate any remaining areas of weakness by reviewing the relevant concepts and strategies that are in your *Cambridge ACT • PLAN • EXPLORE Victrory Student Textbook* and *Cambridge Day Two PSAE Victory Student Textbook.*

DAY TWO PSAE
STEP SIX PROGRESS REPORT
(Student Copy)

The Step Six Progress Reports are designed to help you assess your overall course progress, evaluate your test-taking strengths and weaknesses, and create a study plan that will help you maximize your test score.

DIRECTIONS: Fill out this report with the help of your instructor. Refer to your Step Five Progress Reports for both the Day One PSAE (ACT) and the Day Two PSAE (ISBE-Developed Science, Applied Mathematics, and Reading for Information) to assess how you performed on each test section. (The Day One PSAE forms are located in the *Cambridge ACT • PLAN • EXPLORE Victory Teacher's Guide*, and the Day Two PSAE forms are located in the *Cambridge Day Two PSAE Victory Student Textbook* and *Cambridge Day Two PSAE Victory Teacher's Guide*.) Rank your performance in order to target the areas in which you need the most work before taking the complete PSAE test. Rank your weakest test section as number 1 and your strongest test section as number 7. Then, with your instructor, identify specific skills and strategies to focus on within each test section (*e.g.*, pacing and guessing). Consult your Step One and Step Five Progress Reports for a further breakdown of topic and content areas. Finally, work together with your instructor to identify problems in the textbook, on the CD-ROM, or in your web course that will help you hone the skills necessary to improve in your weakest areas.

Before the PSAE test, work through as many additional review problems as possible in order to perform to your maximum potential on the actual exam. Remember that building and maintaining your skills from now until the date of the exam is essential to obtaining the best possible score.

Transfer this information to the Instructor Copy, and then give that report to your instructor.

Name _____ Student ID _____ Date _____

STUDY PLAN
(Student Copy)

	Test Section	*Rank (1 = Weakest)*	*Strategies and Skills on Which to Focus*	*Additional Review Sections and Problem Numbers*
Science	**Day One PSAE ACT Science**			
Science	**Day Two PSAE ISBE-Developed Science**			
Mathematics	**Day One PSAE ACT Mathematics**			
Mathematics	**Day Two PSAE Applied Mathematics**			
Reading	**Day One PSAE ACT Reading**			
Reading	**Day Two PSAE Reading for Information**			
English	**Day One PSAE ACT English**			

DAY TWO PSAE
STEP SIX PROGRESS REPORT
(Instructor Copy)

The Step Six Progress Reports are designed to help you assess your overall course progress, evaluate your test-taking strengths and weaknesses, and create a study plan that will help you maximize your test score.

DIRECTIONS: Transfer the information from your Student Copy to the Instructor Copy below. When finished, give this report to your instructor.

Student Name _____ Student ID _____ Date _____

STUDY PLAN
(Instructor Copy)

	Test Section	Rank (1 = Weakest)	Strategies and Skills on Which to Focus	Additional Review Sections and Problem Numbers
Science	Day One PSAE ACT Science			
	Day Two PSAE ISBE-Developed Science			
Mathematics	Day One PSAE ACT Mathematics			
	Day Two PSAE Applied Mathematics			
Reading	Day One PSAE ACT Reading			
	Day Two PSAE Reading for Information			
English	Day One PSAE ACT English			

Day Two PSAE

ANSWER KEYS

ISBE-DEVELOPED SCIENCE ANSWER KEY

SECTION ONE—ISBE-DEVELOPED SCIENCE REVIEW (p. 71)

1. C	8. D	15. D	22. A	29. A
2. B	9. C	16. A	23. C	30. A
3. B	10. C	17. B	24. C	31. B
4. D	11. B	18. A	25. A	32. B
5. C	12. A	19. B	26. D	33. D
6. B	13. A	20. D	27. A	
7. D	14. C	21. A	28. A	

SECTION TWO—ISBE-DEVELOPED SCIENCE PROBLEM-SOLVING (p. 77)

1. C	3. B	5. C	7. A	9. A
2. C	4. D	6. A	8. B	10. A

SECTION THREE—ISBE-DEVELOPED SCIENCE QUIZZES (p. 80)

QUIZ I

1. B	4. D	7. B	10. D	12. C
2. B	5. C	8. C	11. C	13. D
3. D	6. B	9. C		

QUIZ II

1. D	4. A	7. D	10. B	12. B
2. D	5. A	8. A	11. B	13. B
3. A	6. C	9. D		

QUIZ III

1. C	4. A	7. A	10. A	13. A
2. B	5. C	8. D	11. A	14. B
3. C	6. A	9. A	12. D	

APPLIED MATHEMATICS ANSWER KEY

SECTION ONE—APPLIED MATHEMATICS REVIEW (p. 96)

1.	C	13.	D	25.	B	37.	E	49.	D
2.	D	14.	C	26.	B	38.	C	50.	B
3.	B	15.	A	27.	D	39.	E	51.	E
4.	E	16.	D	28.	C	40.	D	52.	D
5.	B	17.	B	29.	B	41.	C	53.	A
6.	A	18.	E	30.	D	42.	D	54.	E
7.	E	19.	B	31.	C	43.	A	55.	E
8.	B	20.	C	32.	B	44.	D	56.	A
9.	C	21.	A	33.	E	45.	C	57.	B
10.	A	22.	B	34.	A	46.	B	58.	D
11.	C	23.	D	35.	C	47.	E	59.	E
12.	C	24.	E	36.	A	48.	A	60.	E

SECTION TWO—APPLIED MATHEMATICS PROBLEM-SOLVING (p. 106)

1.	B	3.	A	5.	A	7.	C	9.	E
2.	A	4.	E	6.	A	8.	C	10.	D

SECTION THREE—APPLIED MATHEMATICS QUIZZES (p. 109)

QUIZ I

1.	C	3.	B	5.	B	7.	B	9.	E
2.	E	4.	D	6.	C	8.	A	10.	A

QUIZ II

1.	C	3.	D	5.	A	7.	C	9.	C
2.	A	4.	D	6.	C	8.	C	10.	B

QUIZ III

1.	B	4.	C	6.	C	8.	D	10.	A
2.	E	5.	D	7.	D	9.	B	11.	B
3.	D								

READING FOR INFORMATION ANSWER KEY

SECTION ONE—READING FOR INFORMATION REVIEW (p. 123)

1. C	4. D	7. E	9. B	11. B
2. C	5. A	8. B	10. E	12. C
3. C	6. A			

SECTION TWO—READING FOR INFORMATION PROBLEM-SOLVING (p. 129)

1. C	3. E	5. A	7. B
2. C	4. B	6. D	8. D

SECTION THREE—READING FOR INFORMATION QUIZZES (p. 133)

QUIZ I

1. E	4. A	7. C	9. A	11. B
2. C	5. D	8. D	10. E	12. A
3. E	6. C			

QUIZ II

1. C	3. C	5. C	7. A	9. D
2. B	4. E	6. D	8. C	10. A

QUIZ III

1. D	4. A	6. E	8. B	10. C
2. C	5. B	7. C	9. B	11. B
3. A				